Easy

Spanish

Step-By-Step

A Step-by-Step Guide for Learn Spanish,
Grow Your Vocabulary and Improve your
Skills in the Fun Way

Anthony García

Table of Contents

Introduction

Are you one of those people who have been considering learning a new language? Is Spanish the one you are considering to learn?

In case you didn't know yet, Spanish is one of the most widely spoken languages in the world. More than five hundred million individuals are native Spanish speakers. Therefore, by that figure, it is considered as the second most sought-after language following Mandarin Chinese. Apart from that, a study has shown that it's the most romantic of all languages. No matter if you wish to learn the language simply to widen your knowledge or you simply want to learn it because you're traveling a Spanish-speaking destination, you will require a guide to make your whole learning process much simpler and stress-free.

This book is suitable for you, especially if you're not trying to pass a Spanish class. That's because it will get you speaking the language quick. In any scenario, you don't need to be a language professor just to speak the language. This book will surely teach you how to speak the language with the help of simple and practical examples. It will also walk you through discussions to help you get your point across whenever you are meeting new individuals, finding directions, going shopping, traveling, eating in a restaurant, and so much more. In short, this book will guide you on how to speak Spanish virtually in any sort of situation.

The good thing here is that you won't find boring grammar lessons and rules you wouldn't bother with anyway. As an alternative, you will explore many practical examples as well as notes, which will guide you on how to understand better how to speak. While the Spanish language isn't as complex to learn as English is, the language does have its quirks, you must be familiar.

You will find many reasons for desiring to learn the Spanish language. First, because being bilanguage will make you desirable in the job marketplace. It will also provide you a higher sense of self-confidence if you could step in and assist individuals who are having a difficult time with the language barrier out in public. Have you ever thought of how many instances you've seen somebody speaking the language and having trouble to communicate with other people? You wish you could help them but you can't. Today, you don't need just to stand there. You could finally step in and help both people.

Learning a new language like Spanish is advantageous to your self-value and resume as well. What's more, it is a wonderful way to keep your brain exercising. Some people don't stop learning. Therefore, learning a new language could be your initial step to continuing education.

As you now go on along with the learning journey, you'll discover different vital tips, which make will understanding and speaking the language much simple. Using this book, you could be talking Spanish in no time at all. Best of luck and buen viaje!

A. Method of Learning a New Language

Efficient language learners have a positive response when faced with the unfamiliar. Therefore, instead of letting yourself to feel pissed, confused, and frustrated every time listening to Spanish, why don't you try to keep a positive point of view? Start working to know anything you could. It could help you think of speaking in Spanish as a puzzle to be solved, or it could be an interesting challenge to be reached. Every time you hear spoken Spanish, you must concentrate on what is being told. Do not get distracted by your negative ideas. Listen for cognates that are words, which are similar or almost the same in two languages. Take note that English and Spanish share many cognates. Some of these are much / **mucho**; culture / **cultura**; aspect / **aspecto**; important / **importante**; professor / **professor**; introductory / **introductorio**; and course / **curso**.

B. The Spanish Language

The Spanish language is also called as **castellano** or **español.** This language was established in the Iberian Peninsula in the region of Castile. Spanish is considered as the third most spoken language in the world, according to the United Nations. Approximately, at least half a billion of folks speak the language. It is spoken on four continents and is the official language of twenty nations.

Aside from that, the language is also spoken more every year in the mainland of the U.S. In fact, approximately forty million individuals in the U.S. speak the language at home. That makes up over twelve percent of the population of the country. A 2015 report conducted by a government organization in Spain sowed that there are more Spanish speakers in the U.S. compared there to Spain.

You will find three major differences, which determine how this language is spoken in one region versus another. This includes grammar, accent, and vocabulary. The differences in vocabulary lead in various words utilized in various locations to refer to a similar thing. For instance, the word "the computer" in Latin America is **la computadora**. Meanwhile, you will say it in Spain as **el ordenador**.

When we talk about the accent, you will find some variances among regions. You will also find differences between regions in a similar country. The most evident difference in accent among those Spanish speaker connects to the way to say the letter **z**, the letter **c** then followed by **e** or **i**.

Another example is in Latin America, the letter **z, as well as the letter,** mixes **ci** and **ce** are spoken along with an **s** sound. On the other hand, in central and northern Spain, it was spoken along with **th** sound. For instance, the term for "shoe" is **zapato**. In Latin America, it is uttered as **sapato.** In Madrid, it is spoken as **thapato.**

You might not notice many grammatical differences among regions. However, there are some, which deal with the plural form of "you." In both Latin America and Spain, the term **ustedes** is the formal and plural way to talk "you." Meanwhile in Spain, you will find an informal and plural way to utter "you." **Vosotras** in the feminine while **vosotros** in the masculine. However, **vosotras** and **vosotros** aren't utilized in Latin America. As an alternative, **ustedes** is utilized for the plural "you" in every scenario.

Regardless of such differences in grammar, accent as well as vocabulary, thousands of Spanish speakers converse efficiently across every region where the language is pronounced. Even those speakers of Spanish from various countries understand one another totally well.

C. How to Pronounce the Vowels

Speaking words in Spanish is easier than it is in the English language. That's mainly because if you see a letter in Spanish, you will understand how to speak the sound of that particular letter. The only difficult part of the pronunciation of the Spanish language is that you will find sounds in the language, which do not exist, in the English language. All of them could be hard to speak at first.

Every vowel – **a, e, i, o, u** – make only one sound in Spanish. It is only a quick sound, which remains the same from start to finish,

Here's a detailed example:

- The vowel **A** seen in the typical Spanish term **casa** is the simplest vowel sound to create. The other four vowel sounds concentrate on maintaining the vowel sound brief and constant.
- The vowel **E** creates the sound spoken in the English word "take." You see, it is not pronounced "eyyyy." You do not end it off at the end as we mostly do in the English language.
- The vowel **I** create the sound spoken in the word "fee." It is not "iyyy."
- The vowel **B** creates the sound spoken in "toil." It is not "owww."
- The vowel **U** creates the sound spoken in "rule." It is not "uwww."

D. Pronunciation

Pronunciation is vital in any type of language. Therefore, get the hang of this before you try to talk to someone. Nowadays, it is much simpler, simply because you will find countless videos online that will aid you. In this section, you will learn how to utter individual letters by fitting them into typical, easily spoken Spanish words.

One benefits of Spanish over the English language is that with the majority of words, the pronunciation is phonetic. You see, the words sound as if they're spelled. You will also find some homophones that will puzzle you. Some of those words include "they're," "their," and "there" that sound the same; however, have different spellings and meanings. Below is a brief guide to Spanish pronunciation.

The Vowels

In the Spanish language, you will find five vowels and one sound for every vowel.

[a]	ah	The 'a' is spoken as if you were gargling. Simply open your mouth wide and say as saw and father. Try **mapa, agua.**
[e]	eh	The 'e' sound isn't totally existent in English. The nearest pronunciation might be 'eh' as red and met. You must not say the 'e' as in English. You can try saying **enero**, **verde**.
[i]	ee	The 'i' sound is somewhat similar to 'ee' as bee and feet. You see, the 'i' sound is much different compared to the English pronunciation. For instance, **mi, fino.**
[o]	oh	The letter 'o' is uttered as 'oh.' However, it has a shorter sound as know and boat. You can try **roto, coco.**
[u]	oo	This is pronounced as 'oo' like in do or boot. Try saying **muro, futuro**.

The Diphthongs

In case you didn't know yet, a diphthong is a sound that was made by a mix of two (2) vowels in a single syllable. A sound starts as one vowel and moves to another.

|a|+|i|	ai, ay	The 'ai' and 'ay' sound is like ay and why. You can try speaking **mayo, aire.**
|a|+|u|	au	The 'au' sounds like the expression auch. You can try speaking **aula, aunque.**
|e|+|u|	eu	You will not find a sound for this in the English language. That was something like ew however, with the use of the 'e' sound as bed and the 'u' as do. You can try saying **deudor, Europa.**
|e|+|i|	ey, ei	The pronunciation of 'ey' and ei' is near to say and hey. Try saying **buy, reina.**
|i|+|a|	ia	The 'ia' will sounds like tiara and yah. Try saying **anciano, piano.**
|i|+|e|	ie	The 'ie' sounds similar to yes. Try saying **fiera, tierra.**
|i|+|o|	io	The 'io' is uttered as John or yo-yo. Try saying **rio, radio.**
|i|+|u|	iu	The 'iu' is uttered as you. You can try saying **viuda, ciudad.**
|o|+|i|	oy, oi	The 'oy' and 'oi' sounds similar to boy and toy. Try saying **heroico, hoy.**
|u|+|a	ua	The 'ua' sound is similar to water. You can try saying **aduana, actuar.**
|u|+|e|	ue	The 'ue' sounds similar to wet. Try saying **sueño** and **Huevo.**
u|+|i|	ui	The 'ui' sounds is similar to wheat and we. Try saying **huir, arruinar.**
|u|+|o|	uo	The 'uo' sounds similar to continuous and quote. Try saying **cuota, individuo.**

The Consonants

A series of Spanish consonants are pronounced differently from their English counterparts. If you could, you can try to listen to a local speaker and hear how they deal with them.

[b]	beh	The letter 'b' is uttered after n, m, or l. The sound of this letter is similar to bear and Venice, even though the lips should not touch. For example, **bonito.**
[c]	ceh	The letter 'c' sounds like cereal before i or e. Or else, it might sound like 'k' as computer. For example, **computadora** as 'k' and **cereza** as 'c.'
[ch]	cheh	For example, **chico, chocolate.**
[d]	deh	For example, **dos, dust.**
[f]	effe	The letter 'f' sounds similar in the English fountain or Eiffel. For example, **familia.**
[g]	heh	The 'g' sounds is similar to her before i or e. Or else, it sounds like get or got. For example, **guante** as 'get,' **gesto** as 'her.'
[h]	hache	The letter 'h' in Spanish is silent. For example, **hilo.**
[j]	hotah	The letter 'j' sounds harsh or horse. But never as jump or jar. For example, **jirafa.**
[k]	kah	The letter 'k' sounds similar as in the English language. It is pronounced as key or car. For example, **koala.**
[l]	ele	The letter 'l' is uttered as like or lord. For example, **lobo.**
[ll]	double ele, elle	The double 'l' is spoken as the 'y' in yesterday. For example, **calle**.
[m]	emeh	The letter 'm' is similar as in the English man or mother. For example, **modo.**
[n]	eneh	The letter 'n' sounds similar as in the English note and no. For example, **nosotros.**

[ń|	enyeh	The 'ń' isn't another letter 'n'. This letter sounds as canyon, onion or lasagna. For example, **niña.**
[p]	peh	The letter 'p' is similar to the sound in the English paste or pet. For example, **pelo.**
[q]	koo	The letter 'q' is spoken as curious. If it is written with 'ue' and 'ui' the letter 'u' is silent. For instance, '¿quién?' is spoken as *kien*. What's more, the '¿qué?' as *ke* (using the Spanish 'e'). For example, **qué, quién**.
[r]	ere	The letter 'r' sounds like brr at the start of a word. Or else, it sounds like brown or break. For example, **raton** as 'brr,' **crear** as 'break.'
[rr]	erre	The double 'r' sounds like 'r' at the start of a word. It is sound is much vibrated, as the sound of a vehicle accelerating. For example, **perro.**
[s]	ese	The letter 's' sounds similarly as in the English language sea or sorry. For example, **solo.**
[sh]	esse / hache	The 'sh' sounds as show or shampoo. For example, **show.**
[t]	teh	The 't' sound is pronounced as in English, even though the tongue needs to touch the back of your teeth like test and tea. For example, **tela.**
[v]	veh	The 'v' sounds are proncounced as the letter 'b.' However, your lips are touched slightly as voice or various. For example, **vecino.**
[w]	doble veh	The 'w' sounds have a similar pronunciation as in the English language wine and whiskey. For example, **kiwi.**
[x]	equis	The 'x' sound is spoken as 'gs' or 'ks' like in excited or explosion. For example, **xilófono.**

| [y] | i griega / ye | The letter 'y' is the same as the double 'l.' However, it has a slight difference as yellow and crayon. For example, **yegua.** |
| [z] | setah | The letter 'z' is uttered as 'th' not as in zero or zip. For example, **zorro.** |

Are you now looking for ways to make it simpler for you to say these letters as a native Spanish speaker? Then there's no need for you to worry. You could look online for an audio file and listen to it to make sure you get it all right.

We suggest that you stay away from any translation software when learning how to pronounce any word in the Spanish language. The reason behind this is that such applications do not have the required accent to make you pronounce each word accurately.

Make sure you look for real individuals speaking in the native Spanish language on different video platforms. These people tend to speak authentic Spanish, meaning you could learn more from them and much quicker.

E. Where to Go From Here

The best thing about this book is that you don't need to read them every chapter from the start to the end. Every chapter stands on its own, and it does not oblige you to finish any other of the chapters within the book. That setup saves you sufficient time if you have mastered particular topics but feel somewhat insecure about the others.

Therefore, make sure you leap right in. Now is a perfect time that you get your feet wet. If you not certain exactly where to start, you can look at the Table of Contents. Choose the topic, which appears to best suit your requirements and capabilities. If you are getting concerned that your existing background might not be strong enough, you could begin at the very start. From them, you could work way throughout the book.

Just bear in mind that learning the Spanish language is not a sort of competition. You must work at a pace, which fits your needs. Do not pause to read a chapter a second, third, or even fifth time many days later. Take note that you could adapt this book easily into your learning skills. You need to take note that you should have a positive and confident outlook towards this.

Indeed, you will make some mistakes. Everybody does – in fact; most native Spanish speakers always do. Your goal here is to speak and write. If you could make yourself understood, you have won the greatest part of the war.

F. The Stress Rules

You are already aware that Spanish words are stressed on the *last syllable* when they end in a consonant other than s or n. For example, **Gibraltar, Santander, El Escorial, Valladolild.**

You see, they are stressed on the *syllable before last* when they end in s or n or a vowel. For example, **Valdepeñas, Toledo, Granada.**

When a particular word breaks either of such rules, an accent is written to highlight where the stress falls. For example, **civilización, José, Gifón, kilómetro, Cádiz, Málaga.** Every word ending in –ion bears that accent. Therefore, if you notice a written accent, you should stress the syllable where the accent is located. The only other usage of accents you must understand is that it is situated on *si* to distinguish **si** (yes) from **si** (if).

The only other usage of accents you must understand is that it is situated on *si* to distinguish **si** (yes) from **si** (if).

Colors

Your language learning session wouldn't be complete without knowing how to pronounce and use different colors in a conversation appropriately. It is a significant part of basic vocabulary. With a basic understanding of Spanish colors, you'll find it easier to communicate, make acquisitions, describe and identify things, etc. that are crucial in developing social interaction among Spanish speakers.

Common Spanish Colors

Get to know the most commonly used Spanish colors.

Spanish	English
Amarillo (ROH-hoh)	Yellow
Anaranjado (ah-nah-ran-HA-do)	Orange
Azul (ah-SOOL)	Blue
Azul Marino (a-SOOL ma-reeno)	Navy Blue
Blanco (BLAHN-koh)	White
Cafe (kah-FEY)	Dark Brown
Crema (krema)	Cream
Gris (GREES)	Grey
Marron (mah-RON)	Brown
Negro (NAY-groh)	Black
Rojo (ROH-hoh)	Red
Rosa (RO-sah)	Pink
Verde (BAYR-day)	Green
Violeta (vee-oh-LEH-tah)	Violet
Morado (moor-AH-do), Violeta (vio-LET-ah)	Purple
	Silver
Plateado (pla-te-AH-do)	Gold
Dorado (do-rado)	Light
Claro (KLA-ro)	Dark
Oscuro (os-KUR-o)	

Other Colors in Spanish

Albaricoque	(Apricot)
Alizarina	(Alizarin)
Amaranto	(Amaranth)
Anil o Indigo	(Indigo)
Azul Cobalto	(Cobalt Blue)
Azul de Prusia	(Prussian Blue)
Azur	(Azure)
Beige	(Beige)
Bermillon	(Vermilion)
Blanco Antiguo	(Antique White)
Borgona	(Burgundry)
Carmesi	(Crimson)
Carmin	(Carmine)

Coral	(Coral)
Escarlata	(Scarlet)
Esmeralda	(Emerald)
Esparrago	(Asparagus)
Fucsia	(Fuchsia)
Fucsia Antiguo	(Old Pink)
Glauco	(Glaucous)
Granate	(Garnet)
Gris de Davy	(Davy Gray)
Gris Fresco	(Cool Grey)
Jade	(Jade)
Lavanda	(Lavender)
Lavanda Flora	(Lavender Floral)
Lila	(Lilac)
Limon	(Lemon)
Magenta	(Magenta)
Marfil	(Ivory)
Nieve	(Snow)
Perla	(Pearl)
Piel	(Skin)
Platino	(Platinum)
Rosa Americana	(American Rose)
Rosa Cuarzo	(Quartz Rose)
Sesamo	(Sesame)
Turquesa	(Turquoise)
Vainilla	(Vanilla)
Verde Cazador	(Hunter Green)
Verde Lima	(Lime Green)
Verde Manzana	(Apple Green)
Verde Oliva	(Green Olive)
Zafiro	(Sapphire)

Some of the colors we have here were derived from minerals, flowers, and fruits, like aguamarina (aquamarine), rosa (rose), cafe (coffee), and marfil (ivory).

Some notes about Spanish colors:
- Orange color is called either Anaranjado or Naranja
- Use the term "claro" if you are referring to color with low shade, not including the blue color because the proper way to say "sky blue" or "light blue" is "Celeste."
- Use the term "oscuro" if you are referring to strong color. Examples are *rojo oscuro* and *verde oscuro,* which means dark red and dark green in the English language respectively.

The colors in Spanish work as adjectives and nouns.
- **Nouns:** All of the colors are masculine and singular.
  An example is *"el azul"* (blue)
- **Adjectives:** When describing or saying something about a person or object.

An example is *"el coche azul"* (the blue car).

Spanish Colors as Nouns
When utilized in Spanish, common color names should comply with the nouns they are describing in both number and gender. Some unusual color names, however, are treated inversely in Spanish compared to English. In most cases too, the color names usually come next to the nouns being defined and not before as in English.
The form deviates depending upon the gender and number of what is being described.
Examples:

>*Tengo un coche amarillo* - I have one yellow car.
>*Tiene dos coches amarillos* - He has two yellow cars.
>*Tienes una flor amarilla* - You have a yellow flower.
>*Tenemos diez flores amarillas* - We have ten yellow flowers.

Other common colors include:

>Amarillo (Yellow)
>Azul (Blue)
>Anaranjado (Orange)
>Dorado (Golden)
>Blanco (White)
>Negro (Black)
>Marron (Brown)
>Gris (Gray)
>Rojo (Red)
>Verde (Green)
>Rosa (Pink)
>Purpura (Purple)

Moreover, make sure the Spanish color you'll be using to describe a plural noun must be written in plural forms, such as *verde/verdes* and *rojo/rojos*. For instance, Red Houses are translated as Casas Rojas, which makes both the Roja plural and noun Casa.
Examples:

>*Su libro tiene una portada verde* - Her book has a green cover.
>*Yo tengo un sombrero negro* - I have a black hat.
>*Me encanta tu vestido celeste* - I love your sky blue dress.
>*Esa es una guitarra naranja hermosa* - That is a beautiful orange guitar.

If the Spanish color you intend to use acts as a noun and is followed by a noun, the color could have a plural form, though the adjective or noun should remain in its basic form.
Examples:

>*Los rosas palo no me quedan bien* - Pale pinks do not suit me well.
>*No me gustan los azules marino* - I don't like navy blues.

Also, similar to English, Spanish allows the use of several nouns as colors. Although, the way where they're used as colors greatly differs based on the speaker's preference and region.
Example:

Cafe means coffee and is used to designate a coffee-colored shirt including camisa cafe, camisa color cafe, camisa color de cafe, and camisa de color cafe.

Other nouns that are popularly used in this way as colors include:

Cereza (Cherry)
Chocolate (Chocolate-colored)
Paja (Straw-colored)
Mostaza (Mustard-colored)
Violeta (Violet)
Beige or Beis (Beige)
Grana (Dark Red)
Esmeralda (Emerald)
Oro (Gold)
Malva (Mauve)
Lila (Lilac)
Humo (Smoky)
Turquesa (Turquoise)
Naranja (Orange)
Rosa (Pink)

Name of colors that change with gender:

Orange - Anaranjado/Anaranjada
Yellow - Amarilo/Amarila
Red - Rojo/Roja
Pink - Rosado/Rosada
Black - Negro/Negra
White - Blanco/Blanca
Purple - Morado/Morada
Dark - Oscuro/Oscura
Light - Claro/Clara
Colorful - Colorido/Colorida

Name of colors that DO NOT change with gender:

Orange - Naranja
Blue - Azul
Brown - Marron
Green - Verde
Purple - Violeta/Lila
Gray - Gris
Magenta - Magenta
Maroon - Granate
Turquoise - Turquesa

You can use the words *oscuro* (dark) and *claro* (light) if you want to discuss particular color hues. Use either these two words after another word of color or on their own.

Examples:

Mis pantalones son de color verde oscuro - My pants are dark green.
Mi coche es azul claro - My car is light blue.
El tiene los ojos claros - He has light eyes.

Spanish Colors as Adjectives

In Spanish, colors are also used for describing people, animals, objects, etc. It is important too that the adjectives and nouns should agree in number and gender. The number is either in plural or singular, and the gender is either feminine or masculine.

> *El* is a masculine noun and is used for singular. Ex: *el sofa* (the sofa)
> *La* is a feminine noun and is used for singular.
> *Los* is a masculine noun and is used for plural.
> *Las* is a feminine noun and is used for plural. Ex: *las actrices* (the actresses)

The propensity to name colors for certain objects is more typical in Spanish. Plus, the object-adjective grammar rules are quite different from that of other adjectives.

Additionally, the color adjectives follow and go along with the nouns being modified. But, colors could be changed by added adjectives such as dark green, bright yellow, navy blue, and light green. Once it happens, the color adjective doesn't modify to agree with the noun. It becomes inflexible.

How to Properly Use *Ser* and *Estar*

These Spanish words are two different verbs that mean "to be."

We use the verb *"ser"* when you intend to describe what color something is. Here, you need to make sure the color word agrees with the noun's gender and number since it is still working as an adjective.

Examples:

> *Las botellas son amarillas* - The bottles are yellow.
> *El telefono es negro* - The phone is black.

As for the *"estar"* adjective, it usually denotes to temporary states of being. In rare cases, this verb is used for describing the color of an object or something.

Examples:

> *El cielo es azul* - The sky is blue.
> *El cielo esta gris* - The sky is gray.

Colors that end in *-o*

The group of Spanish colors ending in *-o* includes all of the colors that act similar to standard adjectives. There are two major rules that must be adhered to:
(1) they follow the noun they modify; and
(2) they consist of four forms, and each has four varying endings - feminine singular (ends in *-a*), masculine singular (ends in *-o*), feminine plural (ends in *-as*), and masculine plural (ends in *-os*).

Examples:

> *Juan tiene un mechero blanco* - Juan has a white lighter.
> *El gato blanco esta en la cocina* - The white cat is in the kitchen.
> *Las paredes blancas son aburridas* - White walls are boring.
> *¿Has encontrado el boligrafo plateado?* - Have you found the silver pen?

Colors that end in *-a, -e,* or a consonant

The color names included in this group have no special feminine forms, thereby, not gender-specific. They are just similar to any other colors that work as an adjective.

Examples:

>Tengo unos pantalones azules - I have a pair of blue pants.
>*He perdido el boligrafo rosa* - I have lost the pink pen.
>*Mi hermana ha encontrado una rana verde* - My sister had found a green fog.
>*Las rosas rosas son mi flores favoritas* - Pink roses are my favorite flowers.

Color Words for Human Attributes

In the English language, you usually would not describe a person as having "blonde hair." Except if you're trying to sound poetic. You'd rather say that someone had "yellow hair." The same goes for Spanish language.

Be careful, though, when using colors to describe human attributes. In States, Black, Latino/Hispanic, and White/Caucasian are considered to be three separate races. While in Spanish speaking regions, everyone is a member of a similar race. They call it *la raza*.

Color words are applied to express color variations in the race.

>*Moreno/Morena* - dark-skinned with dark hair and dark eyes.
>*Negro* (though Negrito is most commonly used for polite conversation) - refers to any person of African desert or to an unusually dark Latino.
>*Rubio/Rubia* - often refers to someone whose natural color of hair is lighter than dark brown. It is typically translated as "blond."
>*Blanco* - refers to an actual Caucasian visitor/migrant or an unusually pale Latino.
>*Castano/Castana* - frequently used than the word marron to describe brown hair or eyes.
>*Canoso/Canosa* - used to describe a person with gray hair.
>*Pelirrojo/Pelirroja* - this is used to describe a person with ginger or red hair.

Spanish Phrases with Colors

There are also several phrases that make use of colors when attempting a conversation. Among the most commonly used are:

Christe verde - a vulgar or adult joke (dirty joke). It is the form of a joke that you would never say around your kids, parents, etc. It is also known as a joke with indicative connotations. Aside from *charity verde, humor negro* is also popular among Spanish speaking countries. It is what they call black humor or dark humor in English.

>Spanish: *El siempre cuenta chistes verdes.*
>English translation: He always tells dirty jokes.
>*Velo negro* - means being obstinate about something.
>Spanish: *Veo el futuro negro.*
>English translation: I feel hopeless about the future.

Principle azul - meaning to say the ideal man. Knight in shining armor is its identical English expression.

Spanish: *Sigo esperando a mi principe azul.*

English translation: I'm still waiting for my prince charming.

Media naranja - means to be the other half or significant other of a person.

Spanish: *Por fin encontrado a mi media naranja.*

English translation: I've finally found my other half.

Ponerse morado - this means to eat a lot. It makes use of the similar reflexive verb to that of ponerse rojo. Although, this one differs through filling your face to the point of flare-up.

Spanish: *Me puse morado en la cena anoche. ¡Habia tanta comida rica!*

English translation: I stuffed my face at the dinner last night. There was so much delicious food!

Estar sin blanca - means when younare withoit white or without money. This expression was purportedly came from a coin (known as blanca) that occurred during the fourteenth century in Spain.

Spanish: *Quiero ir al concierto contigo, pero estoy sin blanca.*

English translation: I want to go to the concert with you, but I don't have any money.

Prensa rosa or prensa amarilla - refers to news sources including celebrity gossip, tabloids, and trashy news sources - all of which are below legitimate. Though, *prensa amarilla* talks about to over-the-top, inflated news.

Spanish: *No hagas caso a la prensa amarilla.*

English translation: Don't pay attention to the tabloid news.

So, as you notice, some color words in Spanish do not perfectly match their equivalents in the English language. Brown and purple are generally challenging. Violeta (violet) is common as well. In frequent cases, Spanish speakers translate castano to brown. It is crucial to understand all of the color names as well as the proper way to use them in a sentence or conversation.

Numbers

Making a social interaction with Spanish-speaking people and building a rapport with them wouldn't be possible without proper understanding and usage of Spanish numbers. This guide is intended to help you along the way!

Numbers are everywhere - from the telephone number you have to call in for reservation to the address of a residential property where you are visiting a friend. You have to work out the bill, inquire about the cost of a particular item or food, count to arrange a dinner time, and so much more. It is not enough to produce the numbers; you also need to understand the numbers that Spanish natives or speakers say to you.

Here are the Spanish versions of numbers which you will probably use for future business or travel plans.

Numbers 0-20 in Spanish

0 - Cero
1 - Un, Una, Uno
2- Dos
3 - Tres
4 - Cuatro
5 - Cinco
6 - Seis
7 - Siete
8 - Ocho
9 - Nueve
10 - Diez
11 - Once
12 - Doce
13 - Trece
14 - Catorce
15 - Quince
16 - Dieciseis
17 - Diecisiete
18 - Dieciocho
19 - Diecinueve
20 - Veinte

Examples:

Hay dieciocho personas en la clase. (There are 18 people in the class.)
Tengo dos hijos. (I have two children.)
Yo tengo el numero diez. (I have the number ten.)
La empresa tiene veinte trabajadores. (The empresa has twenty workers.)
¿Tu tienes diecinueve anos? (Are you 19 years old?)
Es catorce de noviembre. (It's the fourteenth of November.)

Numbers 20-100 in Spanish
20 - Veinte
- 21 - Veinteuno, 22 - Veintedos, 23 - Veintetres, 24 - Veintecuatro...

- Note: All of the 20s are a single word.

Examples:
> *El pasaporte es valido por otros veinticinco dias.* (The passport is valid for another twenty-five days.)
> *Mi padre se divorcio cuando tenia veintisiete anos.* (My father got divorced when he was 27 years old.)

30 - Treinta
- 31 - Treinta y uno, 32 - Treinta y dos, 33 - Treinta y tres, 34 - Treinta y cuatro...
- Note: The two words of the 30s are joined by the letter " y."

Examples:
> *El autobus sale dentro de treinta minutos.* (The bus departs in thirty minutes.)
> *Noviembre tiene treinta dias.* (November has thirty days.)

40 - Cuarenta
- 41 - Cuarenta y uno, 42 - Cuarenta y dos, 43 - Cuarenta y tres, 44 - Cuarenta y cuatro...
- Note: The two words of the 40s are joined by the letter "y."

50 - Cincuenta
- 51 - Cincuenta y uno, 52 - Cincuenta y dos, 53 - Cincuenta y tres, 54 - Cincuenta y cuatro...
- Note: The two words of the 50s are joined by the letter "y."

> *Tengo cincuenta y ocho anos.* (I am 58 years old.)

60 - Sesenta
- 61 - Sesenta y uno, 62 - Sesenta y dos, 63 - Sesenta y tres, 64 - Sesenta y cuatro...
- Note: The two words of the 60s are joined by the letter "y."

70 - Setenta
- 71 - Setenta y uno, 72 - Setenta y dos, 73 - Setenta y tres, 74 - Setenta y cuatro...
- Note: There is only one letter difference between 60 *(sesenta)* and 70 *(setenta)*. The two words of the 70s are joined by the letter "y."

Example:
> *Yo peso setenta kilogramos.* (I weigh seventy kilograms.)

80 - Ochenta
- 81 - Ochenta y uno, 82 - Ochenta y dos, 83 - Ochenta y tres, 84 - Ochenta y cuatro...
- Note: The two words of the 80s are joined by the letter " y."

Examples:

> *Mido un metro ochenta.* (I am 1.80 meters in height.)
> *Mi abuela tiene ochenta y tres anos.* (My grandma is 83 years old.)

90 - Noventa

- 91 - Noventa y uno, 92 - Noventa y dos, 93 - Noventa y tres, 94 - Noventa y cuatro...
- Note: The two words of the 90s are joined by the letter "y."

Examples:

> *Naci en mil novecientos noventa y tres.* (I was born in 1993.)
> *Tengo noventa y nueve problemas.* (I've got ninety-nine problems.)

100 - Cien or Ciento

- 105 - Ciento cinco, 145 - Ciento cuarenta y cinco, 165 - ciento sesenta y cinco
- Note: We use *cien* when there's exactly 100 of something, and this number is used before nouns of gender, either feminine or masculine. Examples: Cien plumas (one hundred pens) and cien blusas (one hundred blouses)

  On the other hand, *ciento* is used if you want to produce numbers with one hundred. Examples: 114 (ciento catorce) and 127 (ciento veintisiete)

Numbers 200-900 in Spanish

200 - Doscientos

- 220 - Doscientos veinte, 250 - Doscientos cincuenta

Example: *Aqui establn las llaves de la habitacion doscientos dos.* (Here are the keys for room 202.)

300 - Trescientos

- 325 - Trescientos veinticinco, 330 - Trescientos treinta

Example: *Invite a trescientas personas para la boda.* (I invited 300 people for the wedding.)

400 - Cuatrocientos

- 402 - Cuatrocientos dos

500 - Quinientos

- 513 - Quinientos trece, 560 - Quinientos sesenta

600 - Seiscientos

- 620 - Seiscientos veinte, 689 - Seiscientos ochenta y nueve

700 - Setecientos

- 767 - Setecientos sesenta y siete, 777 - Setecientos setenta y siete

800 - Ochocientos
- 802 - Ochocientos dos, 806 - Ochocientos seis

900 - Novecientos
- 910 - Novecientos diez, 948 - Novecientos cuarenta y ocho

Numbers 1 Thousand to 1 Million in Spanish
1,000 - Mil
2,000 - Dos mil
3,000 - Tres mil
4,000 - Cuatro mil
5,000 - Cinco mil
6,000 - Seis mil
7,000 - Siete mil
8,000 - Ocho mil
9,000 - Nueve mil
10,000 - Diez mil
1,000,000 - Un million

Examples:

¿Cuales son tus planes para dos mil veinte? (What are your plans for 2020?)

Estamos en dos mil diecinueve. (We are in 2019.)

Tengo mil y una razones para no creerte. (I have 1,001 reasons not to believe you!)

Hay cincuenta mil automotiviles en la carretera. (There are fifty thousand automobiles on the highway.)

Be careful when applying for these numbers because they could be tricky. For the 1000 number, you do not say *un mil*. Use only the word *mil* even though it has a "one" word in it. Whereas for 1,000,000 *(un million)*, you cannot count out the *un*.

Gazillion Numbers in Spanish

Numbers bigger than the millions could spin your head a bit. But, don't worry! We're sure you could pull them off in no time! Practice makes perfect, right?

1,000,000 (10(6)) - un million
1,000,000,000 (10 (9)) - mil millones
1,000,000,000,000 (10 (12)) - un billon
10 (18) - un trillon
10 (24) - un cuatrillon
10 (30) - un quintillon
10 (36) - un sextillon
10 (42) - un septillon
10 (48) - un octillon
10 (54) - un nonillon
10 (60) - un decillon
10 (66) - un undecillon
10 (72) - un duodecillon

10 (78) - un tredecillon
10 (84) - un cuatordecillon
10 (90) - un quindecillon
10 (96) - un sexdecillon
10 (102) - un septendecillon
10 (108) - un octodecillon
10 (114) - un novendecillon
10 (120) - un vigintillon
Gazillions - Tropecientos or Chorrocientos millones

Examples:

Tengo un millon doscientos mil quinientos pesos en el banco. (I have 1,200,500 pesos in the bank).

En Chile hay mas o menos trece millones de habitantes. (In Chile, there are more or less 13,000,000 inhabitants.)

En dos mil dieciseis, mas de cuatrocientos setenta y dos millones de personas tienen el espanol como lengua materna. (In 2016, more than 472 million people have Spanish as a mother tongue.)

Also, as you have noticed, the million numbers in Spanish must include the word *"un."* The identical rule also applies for a billion number. Simply add *-es* and then take out the accent if you want to make the plural of billon or millon.

Examples:

2,457,022 - Dos millones cuatrocientos cincuenta y siete mil veintidos

5,382,368 - Cinco millones trescientos ochenta y dos mil trescientos sesenta y ocho

6,986,410 - Seis millones novecientos ochenta y seis mil cuatrocientoz diez

Ordinal Numbers

Ordinal numbers are the ranking numbers, including first, second, third, etc. They are very simple to learn and master, yes, however, there are a few grammatical considerations you have to keep in mind.

First (1st) - Primero
Second (2nd) - Segundo
Third (3rd) - Tercero
Fourth (4th) - Cuarto
Fifth (5th) - Quinto
Sixth (6th) - Sexto
Seventh (7th) - Septimo
Eighth (8th) - Octavo
Ninth (9th) - Noveno
Tenth (10th) - Decimo
Eleventh (11th) - Undecimo
Twelveth (12th) - Duodecimo
Thirteenth (13th) - Decimotercero
Fourteenth (14th) - Decimocuarto
Fifteenth (15th) - Decimoquinto
Sixteenth (16th) - Decimosexto
Seventeenth (17th) - Decimoseptimo

Eighteenth (18th) - Decimoctavo
Nineteenth (19th) - Decimonoveno
Twentieth (20th) - Vigesimo
Thirtieth (30th) - Trigesimo
Fortieth (40th) - Cuadragesimo
Fiftieth (50th) - Quincuagesimo
Sixtieth (60th) - Sexagesimo
Seventieth (70th) - Septuagesimo
Eightieth (80th) - Octogesimo
Ninetieth (90th) - Nonagesimo

Similar to other adjectives, make sure the gender agrees with the object's gender that you are counting. Though, you can likely notice that ordinals exist before the noun they are describing not like other adjectives.

Examples:

El sigundo piso (The second floor)
El piso veinte (The twentieth floor)
La novena nina (The ninth girl)
El novino chico (The ninth boy)
El tercer hijo (The third son)
Los primeros carros (The first cars)
La segunda persona (The second person)
El segundo libro (The second book)
La quincuagesima sexta persona (The 56th person)
El undecimo dia (The 11th day)

Fractions in Spanish

1/2 - una mitad
1/3 - un tercio
1/4 - un cuarto
1/5 - un quinto
1/6 - un sexto
1/7 - un septimo
1/8 - un octavo
1/9 - un noveno
1/10 - un decimo
2/3 - dos tercios
3/4 - tres cuartos

Examples:

Tres decimas partes (Three-tenths)
Una tercia parte (A third)
Una octava parte (An eighth)

How to Tell the Time in Spanish

The way on how to state the time in Spanish is equally the same as that in English, although with a little bit of differences.

When asked: *¿Que hora es?* (What time is it)
You'll say: *Son las cinco.* (It is 5 o'clock.)
Or: *Es la una.* (It is 1 o'clock.)

Remember that time is always feminine; hence, it should be *son las dos* or *es la una*. Add *de la noche* (nighttime or p.m.), *de la manana* (morning or a.m.), or *de la tarde* (afternoon or p.m.) if you want to differentiate between whether it is a morning or afternoon/evening (a.m. or p.m.)

Examples:

Son las dos de la manana (It is 2 in the morning)
Son las dos de la tarde (It is 2 in the afternoon)
Other examples to get you started working with the Spanish numbers:
Son las seis menos cuarto (It is 5:45 or quarter of 6)
Son las cinco y cuarto (It is 5:15 or quarter past five)
Son las cinco y media (It is 5:30 or half past five)

Many Spanish-speakers or Spanish-speaking countries make use of the twenty-four-hour clock. They are saying it as son las catorce (It is 14:00).

How to Tell the Date in Spanish

It may seem a bit complex, but we know it will be a piece of cake for you. In Spanish, there is a pattern when telling the date. You need to state first the day, followed by the month, and then the year.

Example:
17 de junio, de 2015 (17th of June, 2015)

How about if you want to add the week? That's just simple.
It will now become *Jueves 17 de Junio, 2015* (Thursday 17th of June, 2015).
Another thing that differs Spanish language in the English language is that you don't necessarily need capital letters to write the months as well as the days of the week. But, never abridge the date. The year should always be stated as a number. For instance, 1987 is specified as *mil novecientos ochenta y siete*. Plus, you just tell the number in Spanish – no ordinal numbers required for the date (e.g., 1st, 9th, 13th, 20th).

When asked: *¿Cual es la fecha?* (What is the date?)
You'll say: *Es el 17 de junio, 2015.* (It is the 17th of June, 2015.)

How about numbers with a decimal part?

Currently, coma is the only type of delimiter used for separating the integer and fractional part of a decimal number. You should not separate numbers with just 4 digits.

Example:
The number pi 3, 14159 is stated as tres coma uno cuatro uno cinco nueve.

Tips to Practice Spanish Conversation and Vocabulary

Learning the Spanish language is not only about reading books and other reading materials or watching telenovelas and films. There are various ways to expand your abilities in communicating using the language!
To further help you, we have here some essential tips that are guaranteed to help master and improve your skills in Spanish conversation. Make sure to check them out below!

- *Practice. Practice. Practice.*

As the saying goes..."Practice makes perfect." And, this also applies when learning Spanish vocabularies and conversations. Speak as frequently as possible. It is okay to make mistakes once, twice, and many times. That's part of the process. You don't need to kill much of your time engaging in long sessions. Practice at least two to three times every week. Thirty minutes three times per week is enough to yield great results.

Fortunately, opportunities abound. Why not start a conversation with Spanish speakers every time you have the opportunity? Then, use as many of the words you'll learn as possible. What if you're not fully capable of speaking to other people? That's not necessarily a problem since there are other alternatives. Why not talk to yourself in front of a mirror? That could help a lot with your practice.

- **Take notes**

Another great little trick to learn vocabulary and conversation in Spanish is to take notes, especially the words or phrases with difficult meanings. Either has a journal or a small notebook with you every time. Note down all the new words you come across and re-read them all through the week. Doing so will aid you in getting acquainted with the vocabulary and parades as well as implementing them more frequently. Your learning should never stop!

Build a list of key phrases as possible. The initial list must be the one that's particular to the conversation you want to have. Basic Spanish phrases include "What is your name?" "How are you?" and "Where are you from?" Though, consider your phrase lists as your training wheels for learning Spanish. You don't need to memorize them all. Just familiarize yourself with them. That's enough.

- **Act it out**

Writing down notes and speaking with native Spanish speakers or people who know how to speak Spanish fluently is not enough. You also have to put your new Spanish words into motion. This means to act out or do the word or story you're leaning. Just a simple idea: why not perform food word/phrase learning while cooking or in the grocery? The process can be challenging but will be worth it.

- **Find someone or a variety of people to talk with or engage in group conversations**

As we have mentioned earlier, find either a native or experienced Spanish speaker who can help you learn and master both the basics and complexities of every word. After all, the more, the merrier. This would not only help improve your fluency but would also help you make new friends and learn about the cultural facets of speaking Spanish.

Sharing knowledge, taking quizzes, and doing some activities will help both of you keep motivated, dedicated, and engaged in learning. You and your language buddy could also talk about your personal lives, art exhibitions, and other interesting things that will help increase your potential for speaking the Spanish language.

Otherwise, hiring a private tutor can be an ideal solution. Here, you can be able to set your own goals no matter how strict your schedule is and wherever you may be. Several teachers are now specializing in conversational and vocabulary Spanish lessons.

Group sessions, on the other hand, prove to be useful as well since they force you to speak Spanish while simultaneously listening to a group of language learners. They could help you in learning new words and phrases as well as improving your own Spanish quickly. They prepare you for actual social situations in Spanish so that once you're in the same case, you'll end up handling it perfectly.

- **Attend social events**

The main purpose here is to mingle with other Spanish speakers and learn with them for further language improvement. But aside from that, you can also discover some interesting facts about Spanish, its people, history, etc. Social events could be a local art gallery, community meeting, or a cultural event. You will learn about the sentence expressions and structures through observing the Spanish speakers the ways where they try to express themselves in the language.

- **Take advantage of online communities and forums**

The internet is packed with helpful resources for those who want to learn the language of all types, including Spanish. Visit a few online communities and forums to help you out. They feature guides and articles from expert language tutors. Post your question if you can't find the specific answer to your question. Native and experienced Spanish speakers are always glad to give a lending hand.

- **Use learning materials (e.g., flashcards) and reading materials (e.g. magazines)**

We suggest using flashcards during your language practice. Why flashcards? Mainly because it has proven to be an effective tool for learners. Plus, it doesn't need to be expensive and won't kill much of your time. There is a wide range of free apps available both for tablets and smartphones. They will help you create flashcards. Though you can also do it in the traditional way if you want.

If you want the modern way, simply make your own version of flashcards with special extras (e.g., multimedia options and timers). This would make learning as simple as possible for you. Make some that are small enough to carry around. Write English on one side and then in Spanish on the other side.

When it comes to the words or phrases you're going to write on your flashcards, just make it simple first. For instance, focus on things that you usually encounter at home, while shopping, while doing errands, or at work. Examples are *platos* (plates), *cucharas* (spoons), and *cocinar* (to cook). Then, continue with your list.

- **Keep track of your pronunciation and fluidity**

Keep in mind that learning sessions, especially those who take up classes, are intended to improve pronunciation and fluidity. Give out all your focus and do not waste any single valuable time, for example, asking your private tutor or conversation partner to help conjugate in the past tense.

The secret here is to speak more, think less, and discount your errors. Conversation class sessions are more on fluidity; thus, make sure to go with the flow. Later on, you'll find yourself using Spanish vocabulary and conversations like a pro!

How would you address those mistakes during language sessions? Isn't it better to let your doubts known for further improvement? These questions may pop out of your head.

Well, the best solution we could recommend to do is create a note of grammars, words, and phrases you have doubts throughout the session. Then, revisit your notes afterward and look for the answer to your questions by another course. Don't push yourself too hard if you could work them out yourself at a sooner time.

- *Reading short stories could also help*

Reading is learning. Don't worry about the proper pronunciation because the book or other reading materials also include the right way on how to pronounce the words, phrases, and sentences. What makes reading a great alternative way of learning is that it is cheap and effective. Plus, you're also the boss when it comes to managing your time.

It could be texts or books, dictionary, magazines, newspapers, or online articles. These reading materials can revise and inflate your vocabulary. Reading short stories is ideal too, particularly for beginners who want to learn vocabulary in context. Short stories are stay-focused-on and simple to follow. Not to mention, there are tons of places to find short stories, either physical or over the web. Literature and magazines, on the other hand, give you cultural perspectives that you may not able to get from textbooks. There are many Spanish language magazines and newspapers as well as Spanish language literature online. Read whatever suits your interest. Invest five to twenty minutes of your time in reading.

- *Watch videos and films*

If you're a type of person who doesn't involve much in reading sessions and prefer actual alternatives, then watching videos, television series, or films in Spanish could be right for you. Take notice of new phrases or words and look them up either during or after. Among the recommended movies to watch to improve your Spanish vocabulary and conversations are Amores Perros, El Orfanato, and El Laberinto del Fauno.

Make sure the telenovela or films you are watching have Spanish subtitles to better understand and reinforce the language.

- *Consistency is the key*

Remember that learning a language takes commitment and time. All of your efforts wouldn't be paid off if you will not take time to practice all of the methods suggested for you in a continual manner. You can spare a few minutes of your time, but be sure to do the session every day until you're ready enough to show off your Spanish-speaking skills.

- *Be Patient.*

There's no such thing as an overnight result. It is normal to commit mistakes once in a while, especially if you're still in the learning process. No one will dare to judge you. Don't expect to make similar quality of progress day after day and week after week. Sometimes, you might find yourself appearing to make little or no progress at all or struggling. Do not panic or feel embarrassed. Just keep your focus intact.

You are now ready to speak with confidence!

Ordinals

When learning Spanish numbers, people don't forget to include ordinal numbers. Ordinal numbers show the order of thing or events. In simple terms, ordinal numbers refer to qualities, unlike cardinal numbers who talk about quantities.

Both ordinal and cardinal numbers are useful in learning the Spanish language. People who aim to learn Spanish can use ordinal numbers in every speech and conversation.

For example, you can use ordinals while talking about positions or grades. Ordinals also have genders such as masculine and feminine. We'll talk about this later but for now, let's first know the place of ordinals as adjectives.

Ordinals as Adjectives

Ordinal numbers are adjective forms of cardinal numbers.

Here's an example:

Uno or one refers to a cardinal number and *primero* or first is the ordinal form. You also say this for the cardinal number *dos* or two and the ordinal number *segundo* or second.

First time Spanish learners would discover that ordinal numbers are commonly used for numbers under 10. These numbers (that you can also use in Spanish conversations) are as follows:

- First: *primero*
- Second: *segundo*
- Third: *tercero*
- Fourth: *cuarto*
- Fifth: *quinto*
- Sixth: *sexto*
- Seventh: *séptimo, sétimo*
- Eighth: *octavo*
- Ninth: *noveno*
- Tenth: *decimo*

If you're going to use ordinal numbers as adjectives, make sure the numbers agree with the nouns they're referring in both gender and number.

Let me show you:

> El Segundo coche – the second car

> (Here, the Spanish word coche is masculine.)

> La segunda vez – the second time

> (The word vez is feminine.)

Now, what if you're going to use *primero* and *tercero* in a phrase or conversation? The cardinal numbers primero and terecero should precede a masculine noun (singular). Take note: the final -o isn't included in the phrase.

- El primer rey (the first king)
- El tercer trimestre (the third semester).

The change in the phrase is called apocopation.

What's apocopation?

Primero and tercero are shortened or apocopated when these numbers precede a masculine noun (singular). Hence, the numbers turn into primer and tercer.

Take a look at this short sentence:

> Aquel fuel mi primer gran exito.

> (That was my first great success.)

Now, let's say; you're using large numbers, what number are you going to use?

It's simple. Instead of ordinal numbers, you need to use cardinal numbers, particularly in speech. For example, you would use el siglo veinte or the 20th century than el siglo vigesimo, the cardinal form.

Spanish speakers can make a conversation using numerals in this way:

> El siglo 20 is written as el siglo XX.

In general, the 11th and above cardinal numbers are used in formal language often.

Writing Ordinal Numbers Using Superscripted *o* or *a*

The *o* is used when you're talking about masculine nouns. Meanwhile, *a* refers to feminine nouns. So, you would write *2º* instead of 2nd when you tell about a masculine noun. Then, *2ª* refers to a feminine gender.

Gender and Number in Ordinals

Since ordinal numbers are adjectives, ordinals should agree with the gender and number of the nouns they modify. You can speak or write the ordinal feminine form by replacing the ending with -o or -a. The formal structure of these number end in s.

Masculine	Feminine
Primero	Primera
Segundo	Segunda
Tercero	Tercera

Masculine (Plural)	Feminine (Plural)
Primeros	Primeras
Segundos	Segundas
Terceros	Terceras

Abbreviations of Ordinal Numbers

Spanish vocabulary and phrases on ordinals also have abbreviations of ordinals. The two ways to do this are with roman numerals and Arabic numerals. The digits are often followed with ordinal indicators that are or aren't underlined.

Primero, primera, primer	1. $^{\underline{o}}$, 1. $^{\underline{a}}$, 1.	I
Primeros, primeras	1. ^{os}, 1. ^{as}	I

Segundo, segundo	2. º, 2. ª	II
Tercerro, tercera, tercer	3. º, 3. ª, 3. er	III
Cuarto, cuarta	4. º, 4. ª	IV
Quinto quinta	5. º, 5. ª	V

You would notice, there are dots between the numbers and ordinal indicators. Well, the dots are required in writing abbreviations but not in acronyms and symbols. But, you wouldn't use these often in writing basic ordinal vocabulary. It depends on you if you want to include the dot in your texts.

But, the Arabic numerals are often used by Spanish writers. Meanwhile, Roman numerals are commonly used in the following examples. (usually after the noun but except in the las example)

- **In naming centuries**
  Example: Siglo XX (20th Century)

- **In reference to popes, monarchs and emperors**
  Example: John Pope II

- **In enumerating books, chapters, and volumes that have a literary work**
  Example: Capitulo I (Chapter 1)

- **In naming events such as festivals, congresses, etc.**
  Example: La XXII edicion del san Juan de San Juan. (The 22nd edition of the San Juan Film Festival).

As we discussed, you can use ordinal numbers in communicating with native Spanish speakers or foreigners who want to learn Spanish.

What if you want to communicate with people using ordinal numbers more than 10? Here the following ordinal numbers you can use to enrich your vocabulary. You can also use these in making simple Spanish phrases.

- 11th: *undécimo*
- 12th: *duodécimo*
- 13th: *decimotercero*
- 14th: *decimocuarto*
- 15th: *decimoquinto*
- 16th: *decimosexto*

- 17th: *decimoséptimo*
- 18th: *decimoctavo*
- 19th: *decimonoveno*
- 20th: *vigésimo*
- 21st: *vigésimo primero*
- 22nd: *vigésimo segundo*
- 23rd: *vigésimo tercero*
- 24th: *vigésimo cuarto*
- 30th: *trigésimo*
- 31st: *trigésimo primero*
- 32nd: *trigésimo segundo*
- 40th: *cuadragésimo*
- 50th: *quincuagésimo*
- 60th: *sexagésimo*
- 70th: *septuagésimo*
- 80th: *octogésimo*
- 90th: *nonagésimo*
- 100th: *centésimo*
- 200th: *ducentésimo*
- 300th: *tricentésimo*
- 400th: *cuadringentésimo*
- 500th: *quingentésimo*
- 600th: *sexcentésimo*
- 700th: *septingentésimo*
- 800th: *octingésimo*
- 900th: *noningentésimo*
- 1,000th: *milésimo*
- 2,000th: *dosmilésimo*
- 3,000th: *tresmilésimo*
- 4,000th: *cuatromilésimo*
- 1,000,000,000th: *millonésimo*

The examples mentioned above are helpful not only in learning Spanish vocabulary but also in speaking and writing compound ordinal numbers. These numbers involve numerals or digits that are higher than 10.

Here's an example:

You're going to write the compound ordinal number 2365. o

What' s the proper way to write it?

It should be *dosmilésimo tricentésimo sexcentésimo quinto* for the masculine. For the feminine, you would write:

dosmilésimo tricentésimo sexcentésimo quinta or 2365. [a]

What would you write if the numbers are in plural form?

That's simple. Here are examples:

- 31ᵃˢ or (*trigésimas primeras*)
- *Olimpiadas* (the 31st Olympics)

For the numerals 13.° and 29.°, you can write it as two separate words such as *decimo cuarto* and *vigesino quinto* respectively.

Ordinal Alternative Forms

Spanish ordinal numbers have alternative forms that you can also use in learning ordinal vocabulary and phrases. These alternative forms are also considered correct.

Here's a table that shows the most often used ordinal numbers and their alternative forms:

Ordinals	Alternative
Tercero	*Tercio*
Séptimo	*Sétimo*
Noveno	*Nono*
Undécimo	*decimoprimero / décimo primero*
Duodécimo	*decimosegundo / décimo segundo*
Decimotercero	*decimotercio / tredécimo* (obsolete)
decimoctavo...	*decimooctavo...*
decimonoveno...	*decimonono...*

Some Spanish speakers and writers often use fractional numbers (lower 1/10) as if these numbers are numerals.

Some people write el catarceavo instead of the correct one: el decimocuatro piso). So, you need to be careful when you're speaking or writing fractional numbers.

Ordinal Numbers in Sentences

For beginners, it might be little challenging to use Spanish ordinals in sentences. Well, one of the reasons for this is we don't often use ordinals in sentences, unlike cardinals. But, take note that cardinal numbers correspond to the words first, second, third, etc. in the English language. Hence, ordinal numbers are used similarly in Spanish and English.

Take note: most people don't know how to speak ordinals after 10.

Here are the following tips how can you write ordinal numbers in sentences:

Ordinal Numbers Refer to Position or Grades

The word *DECIMO* and ordinal number, such as 1 to 9, is used to write numbers from 11 to 19. Hence, it's an important rule that you remember in using ordinal numbers from 1 to 10.

You can write the ordinal numbers primero and *tercero* as *primer* and *tercer* if these numbers are placed before masculine nouns.

Let's say you're going to write the masculine noun *regalo* in a sentence. The correct way to in include primer or tercer in the sentence would be:

> Mi primer regalo or My first gift.

> But, you can still write primero and tercero in the following sentences:

> Soy el primero or I'm the first one.

> Primero, abra la caja or First, open the box.

Another rule says that you need to use primera and *tercera* before speaking or writing a feminine noun. But, most native Spanish speakers would say:

> Soy la primer taza. In English, I am the first cup.

But, the correct way of saying this sentence would be:

Soy la primera tasa.

If you would notice, we use primera instead of using a primer in the sentence.

Spanish Ordinals Have Masculine and Feminine Gender

As we have discussed above, ordinals could be either masculine or feminine. But, primer and tercer don't have a gender.

Let's say you're going to use *Quinto* in conversation:

Fred: Ella es la quinta.

(She's the fifth one).

Anna: Estoy en quinto granado.

(I'm in fifth grade).

From here, you can see the word "granado" is a masculine noun. Hence, you would observe that ordinal numbers, like adjectives, should agree with the nouns they modify.

How to Make Sentences or Conversations in Spanish Using Ordinal Numbers?

In writing ordinal numbers in sentences to make conversations, most native Spanish speakers use ordinals numbers from 1 to 10.

Why?

Ordinal numbers that are less than 10 are more comfortable to speak and write than numbers more than 10. Even native Spanish speakers have difficulty in speaking ordinal numbers greater than 10.

Let's look at the following examples:

Native Spanish speakers wouldn't say, "I am the 30th". (Soy el trigesimo). But, they would use the phrase such as *EL NUMERO* and a cardinal number.

Hence, we can rephrase the sentence by saying:

Soy el numero trienta.

You would observe that the rephrased sentence version has more sense than the previous sentence. With this, you can make useful phrases and conversations in Spanish such as the following;

Elena: Soy el numero Segundo. (I am the second).

Alejandro: Gracias, Seniorita! (Thank you, Seniorita!)

Remember: Ordinal numbers in Spanish are often placed before nouns.

- El novena libro
- La primera casa

Spanish ordinal numbers also play roles as a subject in sentences, but you need to use definite articles such as the following:

- La
- El
- Los
- A

Sample sentence:

El Segundo es el granador.

(The second one is the winner).

Also, you can speak ordinal numbers in different ways, such as *decimo segundo* or *decimodsegundo*. The word decimosegundo is considered part of the Spanish ordinals by the Royal Spanish Academy in 2005.

How to Remember Ordinal Numbers?

It's wise for beginners to remember cardinal numbers so that it's easy for them to engage in any conversations. Also, it's easy for the person you're talking to understand the words you're saying if you speak the right ordinal number.

Here's an excellent tip you need to take note:

Remember ordinal numbers by connecting these with English words. Take a look at the following:

- The ordinal number primero is related to the English word "primary.
- Segundo is similar to the word "second."
- You can relate tercero with "tertiary.

- Cuarto is similar to "quarter."
- Quinto refers to the number "five."
- Octavo reflects octave that means "eight."
- You can connect the word decimo with the English word "decimal."

For beginners, it's quite challenging to learn Spanish ordinal numbers. But, knowing the ordinal numbers and how these functions help in learning the Spanish language quickly. Once you're familiar with the ordinals, and their roles in a sentence, it's easy to use these phrases in any conversation.

Also, one secret you should know to remember the rules about Spanish ordinals. Yes, it's quite tough from the start. But, as you continue to learn the Spanish language, you would have fun and who knows, you might write a book or poem in Spanish someday.

But, you know what, Spanish ordinal numbers aren't only great ways for you to make excellent conversations. You can also become good at buying stuff from a Spanish online store successfully if you know these ordinal numbers.

So, take time and enjoy learning Spanish ordinals today!

Days and Months

Do you plan to go on a five-week vacation in Spain? Besides knowing Spanish ordinals, you also need to be familiar with the days and months in Spanish. Why?

Knowing days and months in Spanish allows you to plan your trips easily. For example, you schedule your next Spanish destination by looking at the calendar. You can also extend the vacation without difficulty by reading days and months in Spanish touring sites.

Also, you can use days and months in Spanish in making conversations with native Spanish speakers. You can even teach your friends how to speak and read days and months in Spanish.

Are you ready to learn days and months in Spanish? Let's begin.

Unlike its French equivalents, the days in Spanish are easy to remember. Beginners only need to remember: days in Spanish are in small letters, unlike the days in English that are written in upper case letters.

The following are the days in Spanish and their English equivalent:

Spanish	English
Lunes	Monday
Martes	Tuesday
Miércoles	Wednesday
Jueves	Thursday
Viernes	Friday
Sábado	Saturday
Domingo	Sunday
fin de semana	Weekend

Besides these seven days in Spanish, here are other Spanish words that are also related to the days in the Spanish calendar:

- *The day before yesterday*
  (antes de ayer)

- *Today*
  (Hoy)

- *Yesterday*
  (ayer)

- *Tomorrow*
  (mañana)

- *The day after tomorrow*
  (pasado mañana)

You can memorize the days in Spanish to start your journey on mastering the language. You can read the rest of the chapters in this e-book to enrich your vocabulary and phrases in Spanish.

You can spend your vacation in Spain by meeting new friends, and you can use your vocabulary about days in Spanish. Your knowledge in days in Spanish would be your key to enjoy your time in Spain.

Remember: mastering the days and months in Spanish isn't that tough. All you need is the willingness and sincerity to learn the language. It's best to use the simple phases first before you start long conversations.

Take the chance to use the info you learn to enrich your vocabulary skills. With this, you would learn to appreciate the language more.

Months in Spanish

Do you notice the slight similarities between the English and the Spanish months?

Yes, you're correct if you notice that Spanish months are quite the same as the months in English. Also, like days in Spanish, months in Spanish are all in small letters as well.

Here are the months you would see in the Spanish calendar:

Spanish	English
Enero	January
Febrero	February
Marzo	March
Abril	April
Mayo	May
Junio	June
Julio	July
Agosto	August
Septiembre	September
Octubre	October
Noviembre	November
Diciembre	December

Here are example sentences using some of these months:

- Octubre tiene 31 days (October has 31 days)
- Mayo es el quinto mes del año. (May is the 5th month of the year)

What do you notice in the two examples above?

Yes, the months in Spanish are capitalized instead written in small letters. It's a rule that you shouldn't capitalize Spanish months. But, here's the exception, you can capitalize months in Spanish if these are subject of the sentence.

Unlike the days in Spanish, you don't need to use articles such as *El* before months.

In learning months in Spanish, there are a few essential questions that you would hear in a conversation. These following questions are as follows:

- ¿Que mes es este?
  (What month is this?)

- ¿Cual es tu mes favorito?
  (What is your favorite month?)

- ¿En que mes....?
  (What month...?)

On the third question, you would notice the *EN* preposition is used before *QUE*. The word QUE is an essential part of the question because you would still use it to create the answer.

¿En que mes es?

Es en enero

You can say your favorite Spanish month by using Estamos en + mes.

You can say it like this:

Estamos en deciembre.

You would observe that *ESTAR* is the primary or main verb in the phrase. *ESTAMOS* would conjugate ESTAR when you would prefer to months.

For instance, you can use Mi mes favorito es diciembre about your favorite month. But to spice up the phrase, it would be awesome to add *PORQUE* to the sentence.

Mi mes favorito es diciembre porque lleuve.

Now, you would notice that the main verbs in the sentence are *SER* and *ESTAR*.

That's not all.

There are other ways on how can you talk about Spanish months. Here are the most notable phrases you can use:

- *El mes de* that refers to the month
- *Los meses de* that means the months

These phrases are useful when you're describing the events or weather in a particular month.

How Do You Speak the Date in Spanish?

For people who want to learn the Spanish language, saying the date in Spanish is essential. Well, for beginners, you wouldn't be in trouble if you speak the date in Spanish wrong. Yes, your Spanish tutor would forgive you for the simple mistake.

But, it's different when you're talking to native Spanish speakers. The chances are that the people you're talking to wouldn't understand you or they wouldn't be interested in talking to you.

Don't let that ruin your memorable travel to Spain. You can speak dates in Spanish quickly by the [number] of [*month*].

For example, how would you speak 5th of May as the answer to the question of your mother who asks you the date of your interview?

It simple. You would say "el cinco de mayo" that means "five of May" rather than fifth.

Professional Spanish speakers use this in any conversation, but there's an exception – the 1st day of the month.

You can say *el primero de mayo,* but you can also say *el uno de mayo* on certain occasions. For beginners, they need to follow the correct one that is using primero instead of uno.

Here's another example:

> What if you're going to say it's the second of March, how would you say it?
>
> You would say – *es e el segundo de marso.*

Take note: In English, you would say March the 2nd or the 2nd of March. But in Spanish, you wouldn't reverse the word order.

How to Express the Year in Spanish?

Part of Spanish conversations is expressing the year in Spanish. Like the days and months, you also need to make sure that you say or write the year correctly.

Why?

It would be easy for you to make a conversation about dates. If you plan to travel or have a vacation in Spain, knowing to say the correct year would help you book flights and schedule the trip you plan to do.

It's easy to express or say a specific year in Spanish. You only need to use the number itself.

The following are specific years in Spanish and its English number equivalents:

- Mil trescientos quince – 1315
- Mil novecientos noventa y nueve – 1999
- Dos mil – 2000

It's easy to express year in Spanish, so, come now and start practice saying years in Spanish!

Writing Spanish Dates

Dates in Spanish aren't that easy to speak or write. Countries have different norms that make it challenging to write Spanish dates. So, you might be confused to speak or write different dates in Spanish.

Don't worry! You won't get in trouble if you get the dates wrong. But, it's still essential for you to know how to write it correctly. Why?

For instance, you can always see dates pop up when you're traveling to Spain. Let's say you're booking flights to Spain or booking in hotels.

Differences

If you once read Spanish books, you would notice that there are differences in days in Spanish and its English equivalent. This difference enables native Spanish native speakers and (beginners) to make good conversations with each other.

One of the first differences you would notice is that days and months in Spanish are in small letters rather capital letters.

Dates in Spanish are in Cardinal Numbers

English dates are written using ordinal numbers, but Spanish dates are in cardinal numerals.

Here's an example:

Julio Catorce (July 14)

But, there's an exception – you can speak *primero* or first in your phrases such as:

Primero de Marso (1ˢᵗ of March)

Segundo de Agosto (2ⁿᵈ day of August)

Spanish Years are Pronounced as Cardinal Numbers

If you're asked to speak or write years in Spanish, don't forget that Spanish years are pronounced as cardinal numbers.

Here's a good example:

Let's say you're about to read a date in Spanish in your history class.

1455

Your classmate whispers from the back:

Catorce Cincueta y cinco

Say this, and your professor would frown at you. Instead, say:

Mil cuatrocientos cincuenta y cinco.

Now, that's the correct one because you're pronouncing the year similar with cardinal numbers.

Using the Article "El"

In English, we use the preposition "on" to indicate that a particular event happened on a specific date. That's the usual thing we do in writing and speaking dates in English.

Stop if you plan to use the preposition "on" in Spanish.

You see, writing or speaking Spanish dates don't use any preposition but only the article "el." Yes, native Spanish speakers use "el" before a date.

For instance, you would say:

*El 14 de Septiembre es mi cumplea***ños.**

(My birthday is on 14th of September).

Here are other examples you can use to enrich your vocabulary and improve your conversations with professional Spanish native speakers:

Spanish	English
veintinueve de mayo, 2019	29th of mayo, 2019
catorce de agosto, 2011	14th of July, 2011
doce de abril, 1963	12th of April, 1963
dieciseis de enero, 2020	16th of Enero, 2020

Now, you know the basics of speaking and writing dates in Spanish. But, do you know the versions on how you would write a specific date?

Then, let's be familiar with the two versions in writing Spanish days and months. First, you can write dates using the numbers-only version and second, the formal version.

What's the difference between these two versions?

Numbers- Only Version

Like most Spanish speaking countries, the format of this version is ***dd/mm/yyyy***. You would notice that the form is the American style where the month is the first.

Take a look at this:

> September 1, 1990 (American style)
>
> 01/09/1990 (Spanish style)

You would also notice people don't use the numbers-only version in writing Spanish phrases and conversations. But still, you need to know how to write this version. Why?

You can use this version if you're writing dates in Spanish or feel free to share this information with your friends and family.

Formal Version

An important note to remember: the days and months in Spanish aren't capitalized. The basic format in writing the date would be:

[day], el [day]de [month]

For example, you would write the date:

Saturday, May 18, 2017, to sabado, el 18 de mayo de 2017.

You see, most Spanish writers and speakers use the formal version in making conversations in Spanish. Unlike the numbers-only version, the formal version is excellent to include in conversations because you can speak the Spanish days and months. The numbers-only version isn't written in letters but numbers only.

Also, you can use a little variation in speaking dates in the formal version:

Let's take a look at this example:

domingo, el 9 de marso de 2018

domingo, el 9 del marso de 2018

What do you notice from the example?

Yes, you're right! The *de* was written before the year is replaced by *del*. In either way, both the de and del make a correct Spanish phrase if you use these before the year.

Days and months in Spanish take time to learn. But, once you know how to speak or write days, months, and years, you would be able to start good conversations with Spanish speakers.

Is there a secret to learn days and months in Spanish fast?

Yes, and it starts with you!

Relax and take it easy! A makes a lot of courage, patience, and determination to learn the Spanish language. Be passionate and determined in your learning.

People

The Spanish language, like other languages, allows you to interact with people. For example, you plan to go to Spain with your family. Besides the food and scenic places there, meeting and talking with different people is one of the fun ways to enjoy your trip.

Even if don't plan to go there, you can still enjoy your Spanish language learning by making conversations with Spanish speakers.

But don't be excited yet.

You need to prepare first, So, here are common "people words" that are essential to add to your vocabulary.

People Words

El bebe	Baby
El muchacho El chico	Boy
La muchacha La chica	Girl
Los niños	Children
El amigo La amiga	Friend
La señora	Lady
La anciana	Old woman
El hombre	Man
El anciano	Old man

La mujer	Woman
El niño	Young boy
La niña	Young girl
La señorita	Young lady
El adolescente, la adolescente	Adolescent
El señor	Gentleman
La gente	People

Take time to memorize these words for you to have a basic vocabulary of the common words that refer to people in Spanish. If you hear these words in a conversation, it's would be easy to understand the conversation.

Don't forget – the people you're talking with would be happy to share more ideas and even stories with you.

What if you're asked to describe yourself or someone in Spanish, what words are best to use?

Don't worry!

Enrich your vocabulary more with the following words:

Agil	Agile
Afectuoso	Affectionate
Aburrido	Boring
Agradable	Pleasant
Amable	Kind
Alegre	Joyful
Ambicioso	Ambitious

Amoroso	Loving
Amigable	Friendly
Apatico	Listless
Atrevido	Sassy
Atento	Attentive
Curioso	Curious
Considerado	Considerate
Directo	Direct
Discrete	Discreet
Elagante	Elegant
Hermoso	Beautiful
Horrible	Awful
Insensible	Insensitive

These examples are only a few of the many words you can use in a conversation with a native Spanish speaker. But, there are instances where you find these words useful in the following scenarios:

- If someone asks you about your family and friends
- If you would discuss your favorite film
- If you're looking for someone
- If you're in a clinic or hospital in Spain

You can describe your personality in Spanish by saying Yo soy (I am). In describing another person, use *el* for man and *ella* for a woman. You can use *ella es* besides ella in your description.

Here are a few examples:

- Soy alegre (I'm happy)
- Ella es amigable (She is friendly)

- El es amoroso (He is loving)
- Soy bien ambicioso (I'm very ambitious)

Common Spanish Adjectives Used to Describe People Around You

Like most languages, the Spanish language also has commonly used adjectives to describe people (such as friends and family).

Besides the list above, here are other Spanish adjectives that can enrich your vocabulary and help you create good conversations with newbie and pro-Spanish speakers.

Feliz	Happy
Lindo	Pretty
Feo	Ugly
Alto	Tall
Triste	Sad
Grande	Big
Bajo	Short
Pequeño	Small
Complicado	Complicated
Simple	Simple
Divertido	Fun
Fiel	Loyal
Rico	Rich
Pobre	Poor

Repugnante	Disgusting
Delicioso	Delicious
Intelligente	Intelligent
Tonto	Stupid
Viejo	Old
Nuevo	New
Abierto	Open
Cerrado	Closed
Cansado	Tired
Caluroso	Hot
Desprierto	Awake
Frio	Cold
Rapido	Fast
Lento	Slow
Tranquilo	Tranquil
Loco	Crazy
Debil	Weak
Fuerte	Strong
Enfermo	Sick
Dulce	Sweet
Sano	Healthy
Limpio	Clean

Sucio	Dirty
Mojado	Wet
Injusto	Unfair
Seco	Dry
Justo	Fair
Vacio	Empty
Lleno	Full
Delgado	Thin
Gordo	Fat
Bueno	Good
Malo	Bad
Torpe	Clumsy
Timido	Shy
Valiente	Brave

Do you notice the Spanish word **simple** has the same spelling with its English equivalent? Now, you would ask:

How do you I pronounce it?

It's easy! Take note that the Spanish simple has a stress on the beginning. In English, you put the stress at the word's end.

For example:

The stress on the word is in the first syllable like SIM-ple (SEEM-pley). In English, you pronounce the word as sim-PLE (sim-PULL).

Simple isn't only used to describe a person but also food. Why? The word simple has a connotation of lacking or bland. Most people use *simple* to describe what they think of the food they ate.

Now, read the word **abierto**.

If you aren't familiar with the word, you would think that It refers to an establishment or shop. But, it can also describe a person.

Let this example show you:

>Es Una persona muy abierta.

>(He or she is a very open person.)

>Now, we go to the Spanish word **tranquilo**.

At first, you would use this as an adjective that means tranquil or calm. But, did you know that the word can also refer to order or suggestion?

For instance, you say tranquilo to your angry friend. The word doesn't only mean to relax or calm down but also mean the assurance that things would be alright. You say the word in a calm tone and your friend would get the message.

What do you think about the word **dulce**?

No, dulce doesn't pertain to flavor but also a compliment. In saying dulce to describe a friend, you're saying about your friend's sweet nature. Hence, you would say:

>Eres dulce. (You're sweet.)

The person you're talking to might use dulce to describe sweet candy on your feet. Thus, the person would describe the candy's sweet taste instead of referring to your personality.

>Esta dulce.

Take note: using ser and estar change the meaning of dulce from a personality trait into a flavor.

Making Spanish Conversations with People

Before we start with the conversation proper, let me share a few ideas about the Spanish culture.

The culture in Spain is a cheek-kissing culture, so expect that you would kiss and be kissed on the cheek often. It doesn't mean that a person likes you, but it only shows politeness.

You can also be polite a person by saying Spanish phrases such as the following:

- **Buenos dias (**Good morning)
- **Buenos tardes** (Good afternoon)
- **Buenas noches** (Good night)

Then, you can start the conversation by saying the following:

- ¿CÓMO SE LLAMA? **(You can translate this to "What do you call yourself?" or "What is your name?"**
- ME LLAMO + NAME (MY NAME IS__)
- MUCHO GUSTO (OR NICE TO MEET YOU)
  THIS PHRASE MEANS THAT YOU'RE PLEASED TO MEET THE PERSON. IN SPAIN, THIS PHRASE IS THE STANDARD RESPONSE YOU WOULD HEAR FROM A NATIVE SPANISH SPEAKER.
- ¿CÓMO ESTÁ USTED? (or How are you?)
  You would hear this often in talking to a Spanish speaker. The polite way to answer this is to say bien (good) or muy bien (very good).

Using Spanish vocabulary and phrases, you can get into a small talk easily. Most cultures have this (not only Spain). A small talk enables people to relax and enjoy the casual moment of meeting someone for the first time.

When you're talking to strangers, it's good to be courteous because this marks an excellent conversation together.

Don't ask a person who's out in the rain questions like, "What are your favorite hobbies? Or "How much is the food here?"

The person you're talking to might get annoyed and wouldn't have the interest to start a conversation with you. Instead, you say the following phrases to lighten up the mood:

- Gracias (Thank you)
- De nada (You're welcome)
- Lo Siento (Sorry)
- Disculpeme

Getting to Know People in Spanish

One of the awesome things about learning foreign languages such as Spanish is you get to know about other people! Your Spanish language skills allow you to meet and talk with different people. You share your ideas with them an vice versa.

Once you get to know a person, you can create friendships and much more. But, you need to know the essential phrases to start the conversation,

The following are examples of the phrases you can say:

- ¿QUÉ? (What?)
- ¿A QUÉ SE DEDICA? (or What is your job?)
- ¿DÓNDE? (Where?)
- ¿DÓNDE VIVE? (or Where do you live?)
- ¿DE DÓNDE ES? (meaning Where are you from?)

Alright, you did good in asking questions, but what are your answering phrases if you're asked questions in Spanish?

Don't worry!

Here are a few answer phrases you need to know:

- SÍ. (Yes.)
- NO. (No.)
- (YO) TENGO TREINTA AÑOS. (or I am 30 years old.)
- SOY INGENIERO. (meaning: I'm an engineer.)
- ME GUSTA BAILAR. (I like to dance.)
- ME GUSTA (I like)

When you're about to end the conversation, don't leave abruptly. Remember: talking to a person or people means you need to be polite even if you're about to say goodbye. Still, you need to be courteous and polite to your acquaintance or a new friend.

What are the common phrases you have to say?

Take a look at these examples:

- ¿QUÉ HORA ES? **Or** (What time is it?)
- ME TENGO QUE IR. Or (I have to go.)
- HASTA LUEGO. (See you later.)
- HASTA PRONTO. (See you soon.)
- CUÍDESE. (Take care.)

- ADIÓS. (Goodbye.)

You can mention the important things you need before you exit. It's best to say these in 15 minutes. Like other conversations, you exit by wishing the person well and promise you would see each other again.

Remember: It's okay to make mistakes in making a conversation in Spanish. We're not perfect, and there's always room for improvement. If you're talking to a pro-Spanish speaker, he or she won't bother at all as long the conversation is fun.

Don't give up in learning about Spanish vocabulary and phrases in talking to people. It's tough from the start, but soon, you would speak Spanish like a pro, especially if you know how to ask personal information. (that would be discussed below)

Asking and Giving Personal Information

Let's say you've met someone in a restaurant and you start to make a conversation.

What possible questions you should ask? What answers would you give if you're asked common questions? You read the examples below for you to start and end the conversation successfully.

Before you start the conversation, don't ask personal questions but unique ones about the person or people.

Spanish Questions	English Equivalent	Answers	English Equivalent
¿Cómo se llama? *(formal)*	What's your name?	*Me llamo...or Mi nombre es...*	My name is...
¿Cómo te llamas? *(Informal)*			
¿Cómo está? *(formal)*	How are you?	*Estoy bien, gracias.*	I'm fine, thank you.
¿Cómo estás? *(informal)*			

¿Cuántos años tiene? (formal)	How old are you?	*Tengo X años.*	I am X years old.
¿Cuántos años tienes? (informal)			
¿De dónde eres? *¿De dónde es?*	Where are you from?	*Soy de España.*	I'm from Spain.
¿Tiene hermanos? (formal)	Do you have any siblings?	*Sí, tengo un hermano.*	Yes, I have one brother.
¿Tienes hermanos? (informal)			
¿A qué se dedica? (formal)	What do you do for a living?	*Soy médico/a.*	I'm a doctor.
¿A qué te dedicas? (informal)			
¿Cuál es su número de teléfono? (formal)	What is your phone number?	*Mi número de teléfono es...*	My phone number is...
¿Cuál es tu número de teléfono? (informal)			
¿Está casado/a? (formal)	Are you married?	*Sí, estoy casado/a.*	Yes, I'm married.
¿Estás casado/a? (informal)			

*Take note: The Spanish questions use both **tu** for the informal and **usted** for the formal options. You would need to use either of these options depending on the people you're talking to and the situation.*

In Spain, tu is often used on many occasions, But, if you're in Latin American countries, usted is often used in talking to strangers.

Conversations with people are fun if the questions are about hobbies or interest. If you want to enjoy the conversation, here are a few questions you might ask and its answers:

Spanish Questions	English Equivalent	Answers	English Equivalent
¿Tiene un hobby? (formal) ¿Tienes un hobby? (informal)	Do you have a hobby?	Me gusta cocinar	I like to cook.
¿Tiene una mascota? (formal) ¿Tienes una mascota? (informal)	Do you have a pet?	Sí, tengo un gato.	Yes, I have a cat.
¿Le gusta la música? (formal) ¿Te gusta la música? (informal)	Do you like music?	Sí, me gusta el jazz.	Yes, I like jazz.

English Equivalent	Answers	English Equivalent
Do you have a hobby?	Me gusta cocinar	I like to cook.
Do you have a pet?	Sí, tengo un gato.	Yes, I have a cat.
Do you like music?	Sí, me gusta el jazz.	Yes, I like jazz.

There are other questions you can ask that are about movies, pastime and more. Don't out-Spanish the people you're talking to even if you're Spanish vocabulary improves. It's okay to be natural and casual around people.

Think that you're talking to your friends to make the conversation light and funny. Keep in mind that good conversations start with you, so make it memorable!

Family & Relatives

Family is considered one of the primary topics of conversation, which will come about when you come across Spanish-speakers. In Hispanic culture, plays a vital role, and new Spanish-speaking friends and associates are always interested in knowing about your whole family, too. If you're young, be ready to tell about your mom and dad, and siblings- their jobs, their age and their residences as well. If you look old enough to have kids, look forward to talking about them or enlighten why you do not have any yet. It is a smart idea to have pictures to spark your conversation.

One thing which makes learning Spanish vocabulary about family is a bit easier, and stress-free is the fact that sometimes instead of learning varying words for the male or female family members, you can alter the ending. The masculine plural version is able to be used to refer to many females and males. The only time you would utilize the female plural version is when the group is composed of all female.

Sexual Category and Members of the Family

Always remember that In Spanish, the plural form of a male can refer to varied groups of females and male. As a result, "cuatro hijos" can be signified either four children or four sons; it all depends on the context.

While it might sound odd to the ear adjusted to English language, padres is a grammatically correct way to refer father and mother, even if padre is only referred to a father. Keep in mind also that the phrase pariente in general means "family members or relative"; the cognate, which is a Spanish-English word, does not just refer to parents.

Here are Some of Family Vocabularies in Spanish

el padre	father
los padres	parents
el papá	Dad or daddy
la mamá	Mom or mommy
la madre	mother

el hija	Daughter
la hijo	Son
los hijos	children (males and female)
el esposo or marido	Husband
la esposa	Wife
el hermana	Sister
la hermano	Brother
los hermanos	siblings (male and female)
El arbol genealogico	Family tree
El bisabuelo	Great grandfather
El bisnieto	Great grandson
La conuge	Spouse
El cuatrillizo	Cuadruplet
El quintillizo	Quintuplet
El septillizo	Septuplet
El sextillizo	Sextuplet

Spanish Vocabulary of Extended Family

Countries that speak Spanish, the extended family is very significant. Therefore, it is good to have a firm and thorough understanding of the vocabulary and the terms of extended family. Here are some of the Spanish vocabularies of extended family.

los parientes	relatives
el abuela	grandmother
la abuelo	grandfather
los abuelos	grandparents
el nieta	granddaughter
la nieto	grandson
los nietos	grandchildren
el tía	aunt
la tío	uncle
los tios	aunt(s) and uncle(s)
la prima	cousin (female)
el primo	cousin (male)
los primos	cousins (male and female)
el sobrina	Niece
la sobrino	Nephew
los sobrinos	Both nieces and nephews

Spanish Vocabulary of the Mixed Family

At this point in time, the blended family is turning out to be the norm. In case you have a mixed family, it's a smart idea to learn the vocabulary which pertains to you to precisely illustrate the makeup and composition of your family.

Here are some examples of Spanish vocabulary of the mixed family:

el padrastra	stepmother
la madrastro	stepfather
los padrastros	stepparents
el hijastra	stepdaughter
la hijastro	stepson
los hijastros	stepchildren
el hermanastra	stepsister
la hermanastro	stepbrother

los hermanastros	stepbrothers and stepsisters
el medio hermana	half-sister
la media hermano	half-brother

Spanish Vocabulary of the In-Laws

If you're married, you might find that you spend most of your time talking about your in-laws. Many *in-law* terms are complicated compared to other family vocabularies, so begin by learning the basic which you utilize most often prior to knowing the additional terms and phrases.

Here are the examples of Spanish vocabulary of the in-laws:

el suegra	mother-in-law
la suegro	father-in-law
los suegros	mother and father-in-law
el yerno	son-in-law
la nuera	daughter-in-law
el cuñada	sister-in-law

la cuñado	brother-in-law

TIP: *Don't be persuaded to utilize the term paYiente to refer to parents as it signified relatives, anyone who is related to you. The phrase Los padres may look like an odd way of referring to el padre or la madre. However, it is, without a doubt, the right word for "parents." You can make use of the word la familiapolitica to refer to in-laws.*

Family Vocabulary in Plural Form

Female	Male	Plural
adre [mother]	La mEl padre [father]	Lospadres [parents]
La hermana [sister]	La hermano [brother]	Loshermanos [siblings]
ija [daughter]	La hEl hijo [son]	Loshijos [children]
La abuela [grandmother]	El abuelo [grandfather]	Losabuelos [grandparents]
El nieta [granddaughter]	La nieto [grandsone]	Lasnietas [grandchildren]
LatÃa [aunt]	El tÃo [uncle]	LostÃos [aunts and uncles]
La sobrina [niece]	El sobrino [nephew]	Los sobrinos [nieces and nephews]
La prima [female cousin]	El primo [male cousin]	Los primos [cousins]
El esposa [wife] La mujer [wife]	La esposo [husband el marido [husband]	

La suegra [mother-in-law]	El suegro [father-in-law]	Los suegros [parents-in-law]
La cuñada [sister-in-law]	El cuñado [brother-in-law]	Los cuñados [siblings-in-law]

Some members of the family or relatives can be called in many ways. Like for instance, you can make use of papa/padre for a dad/father or a mama/madre for a mother in Spanish. In general, children usually call their parents papa and mama. Always bear in mind that these two phrases require the accent on the last syllable, or when to pronounce in a different way will have a totally new meaning.

The term "padres," a generic name for parents, it is also the plural form of a gather. See that the phrase parentes means members of the family or relatives. So, you do not make mistakes in Spanish and make use of it if the topic is your parents. We have already mentioned the Spanish term for sister and brother above, Hermana and Hermano. Hermanos is the generic name for them.

If you wish to learn simple and basic Spanish and speak to your grandmother and grandfather, you need to make use of Abuela or Abuelo, which has a generic name of abuelos. On the other hand, there's also a sweet way to address your grandparents in Spanish. You simply put in the suffix "ito" at the end of the phrases, and you will get abuelita and abuelito.

As you see, the female noun which portrays a family in Spanish normally ends in A. On the other hand, words that have -0 at the end are regarded as a male noun. Like for instance:

Niece – Sobrina

Mother-in-law in Spanish – Suegra

Cousin (female) – Prime

Sister-in-law in Spanish – Cuñada

Cousin (male) – Primo

Nephew – Sobrino

Brother-in-law – Cuñado

Father-in-law – Suegro

Only some transformations with the phrase ending, and you will get another meaning. The only exception is the term papa who has a word ending. However, it still utilized for a father or dad in Spanish.

Family Relationships Spanish Vocabulary

Possessive Adjectives Forms

	Singular	Plural
My	**MI**	**MIS**
Your (Familu)	**Tu**	**Tus**
Her, His, Its, Your	Su	Sus
Our	Nuestro/a	Nuestros/as
Your (fam.)	Vuestro/a	Vuestros/as
Their, Its, Your	Su	Sus

Possessive adjectives such as Mi (s) (my), Tu (s) (your), nuestros (s) (our), SU (s) (his, her, their) are normally utilized to refer to family relationships in Spanish. These phrases state possession and should agree in number and gender with the member of the family you like to discuss with. To put it in another way, if you like to know conversational Spanish and say My mom in Spanish, you will say Mi Mama. On the other hand, if you want to say, my brothers, you must make use of MIS instead of MI.

How to Describe a Member of the Family with Ser

Describing your loved ones to your Spanish friends is not a hard and complicated task. To successfully do it, you just keep in mind four important things; relatives or a family member you are planning to describe to talk about, right possessive adjective, the irregular verb SER as well as adjectives to portray physical appearance as well as personality in Spanish.

Irregular Verb SER

The infinitive form of SER stands for "to be"

As a guideline, make use of this verb to discuss inherent features or permanent states such as:

The traits or characteristics of a person

Things that will not change, such as family members and gender:

> She is my mother –Ellas Es Mi Madre

> I am a person- Yo Soy Una Persona

> You are tall – Tu eres alto

In general, the irregular verb SER is utilized in different forms; like if you like to discuss single person and son for many members of the family. Like for instance:

> My father is—Mi Padre es...

> My Mom Is- Mi Madre es

> My cousins are --- Mis Prismon son...

After the right form of verb SER, you must make use of an adjective like amiable or kind or titles of the job such as teacher (professor). To make the adjective stronger, never forget to utilize adverbs such as MUY, which means "very."

Varied Family Terms in Spanish

Los politicos or la familia politica might be utilized as the counterpart of the in-laws. In other terms, the words refer to those to whom you are connected by marriage. In a diverse context, the word politicos also refer to politicians.

The word amigovia or amigovio can be utilized colloquially in most areas to an individual with whom you have a sexual or romantic relationship which has not necessarily been honored or formalized like friends with benefit, or live in lover wherein there is not necessarily a hope or anticipation of getting married. This is a term of relatively recent origin; therefore, its meaning is not consistent in all aspects.

Keep in mind that while the term marido means a husband, there's no equivalent female form marida, in regular use.

Here are Some Helpful Expressions to Discuss Family Relationships

TENGO **plus number plus siblings or uncles or aunts and many others**

Like for instance: Una hermano y dos hermanos, tengo tres hermanas, I have three siblings, one brother, and two sisters.

MI FAMILIA **plus** ES **plus adjective** → **my family plus is plus adjective**

Here is an example: Mi familia es muy grande. → My family is really big.

PRESENTAR A ALGUIEN → TO INTRODUCE SOMEONE

Like for example: TE PRESENTO A MI ESPOSA. → I present you to my wife

ÉL/ELLA **plus** ES **plus relationship to you** → **he/she plus is plus relationship to you**

Like for example:

ÉL ES MI TÍO. → He is my uncle.

TIP to Remember: *Keep in mind, we virtually always make use of possessive pronouns like tu, su, mi, sus, vuestro/a/os.as, nuestro/a/os/as when discussing members of the family.*

To give you an insight; please take a look at these examples:

They are my grandparents- Ellos son nuestros abuelos
She is his or her aunt- Ella es su tia
To look like someone- parecerse a alquien

Example:

Randy looks like his father- RANDY SE PARECE A SU PADRE.

There's a high chance that the following Spanish discussion which you hear or participate will talk about members of the family. Ensure to take the time to get to know more about the vocabulary to discuss members of the family because it will surely be put to good use!

Sample Sentences which refer to members of the family

Here are simple sentences you are able to utilize as models for your own:
My dad is a carpenter – Mi padre es carpintero
My auntie is a dancer- Mi tia es ballerina
My mom is a housewife- Mi madre es ama de casa
I have three sistsers and a brother- tengo tress hermanas y a harmano

Tengor cuatro hermans. This can be viewed as vague and uncertain by English speakers. It could be translated correctly as either I have 4 siblings or I have 4 sisters.

Tengo singko tias – I have five unties or I have five uncles and aunties

Mi madrastro vive en el estado de Texas- My stepdad lives in Texas State.

Mis sobrinas viven in US- My nieces live in the US

Mi madre esta muerto - My mom is dead.

Mi primo esta muerta - My make cousin is dead

John y Carol fueron los padres de Elisa - John and carol were the parents of Elisa

Los primos no pueden casarse según nuestra cultura - Cousins can't marry according to our culture

Directions

Your Linguistic Guide to Directions in Spanish

Have you lost while you're travelling a country or around a city? Losing yourself in a new place and country is a thrilling way to travel around! On the other hand, if you decide to go back to your hotel to take rest, it can be a challenge to look for your way, most particularly when there is a language difficulty to assert with.

Fortunately, this is a simple issue to address if you are spending your holiday in Spain or other Spanish speaking nations. Knowing how to speak directions in Spanish is indeed a very simple thing to do. With a little effort and time, you are able to know how to give and ask for directions in Spanish like you're living in the locality.

If you decide to spend a vacation in a Spain or other countries where Spanish is the primary language, you must allocate more time to evaluate how to give and ask for directions in Spanish. You will thank yourself the very first time you lost, and although you have a smartphone or a map to help you find the way, asking for directions is indeed a good way to practice the Spanish language with locals.

Even when you do not have a plan of travelling in Spanish speaking countries, giving and asking directions is Spanish still a practical skill which is worth learning. Keep on reading for directions vocabulary, practice suggestions as well as useful phrases.

The Importance of Learning Directions in Spanish

Knowing how to give and ask directions in Spanish is extremely useful than what many people think. Going to a country with the Spanish language? Asking for a direction is perhaps the most common conversation you will have in Spanish, most especially if you are not skilled in using a map.

And it is not only vital to learn how to give and ask for directions in Spanish. If you aren't able to understand the answer, then you will also be lost. Learning the grammatical structures and vocabulary in this guide could make a huge difference between looking for a destination and being lost hopelessly on holiday.

What is more, knowing more about directions is indeed great due to the fact that it will enable you to practice many new vocabularies and it pressures you to listen and focus on difficult prepositions as well as configurations of the verb in the form of command. Below is the list of vocabulary that is broken down into nouns, verbs, adjectives as well as prepositions.

Important Vocabulary Phrases for Directions in Spanish

This list of vocabulary has lots of useful phrases/words related to directions in Spanish.

Nouns

- Avenue- la avenida
- Street- la calle
- Alleyway- el callejon
- Highway- la carretera
- Bridge- el Puente
- Pedestrian street- la peatonal
- Sidewalk- la vereda/ la acera
- Ma- el mapa
- Roundabout- la rotunda
- Stoplight- el semaforo
- Crosswalk- el paso de peatones
- Directions- las direcciones
- Address- la direccion
- Block- la manzana/ la cuadra
- Mile- la milla
- Kilometer- el kilometer
- The right (hand/side)- la derecha
- The left (hand/side)- la izquierda

Adjectives

- Right- derecho, derecha
- Left- izquirdo/a
- Straight (when describing physical appearance)- recto, recta, derecho, derecha
- Next- proximo, proxima
- First- primero, primera
- Second- Segundo, segunda
- Third- tercero- tercera
- Near- cerca
- Far- lejos
- Lost- perdido- perdida

87

Deracha and derecho are two easily confused Spanish words. Both are a distant relative of the words direct and right, and which is the main source of the uncertainty; depending on the use and context of these terms can give meanings like the *right (entitlement)*, *right (opposite of left)*, directly, straight, and upright.

Derecah and Derecho Explained

These terms are easiest to comprehend as nouns:

El dereche isn't an expression of direction. It is utilized to explain something which is due to a person in accordance with the law, custom or moral principle. When this word is utilized in plural form, usually it means rights like in the saying derecho humanos, or human rights. Also, it can refer to a kind of right which is less abstract.

La derecha, on the other, refers to something which is on the right side of opposite of left, like for instance, the political right or the right foot. A la derecha is an advervial term which means on the right or to the right.

Here are Sample Sentences to Avoid Confusion:

> *Queremos el **derecho** a decidir para toda la gente* - We want the right to decide for all the people.)

> *El coche es caro, pero no me funciona la luz de cruce **derecha**-* The car is expensive, but the right turn signal does not work for me.)

Prepositions and Direction

Prepositions are utilized in virtually every sentence. They can be a remarkable tool to connect words. Like for instance, by just understanding how to make use of with, after, from, to, you are able to expand the scope of the conversation. In short, preposition explains a connection between phrase in a sentence.

Grammar Rule

In Spanish, prepositions are utilized the same way they used in English. To make life easier for Spanish learners, check out some of these examples:

- *The hat is under the table- El sombrero está <u>debajo</u> de la mesa.*
- *I like tea with milk- Me gusta el té <u>con</u> leche*

List of Preposition in Spanish

- Until- hasta
- Forward- adelante

- In front of- delante de
- Behind- detras de
- Nex to- al aldo de
- Across from- en frente de

Some Examples

- *La carta esta dentro del libro- The letter is inside the book*
- *¿Le puedo ayudar?¿Le puedo ayudar?- Can I help you?*
- *La pluma está debajo del escritorio- The pen is under the desk*

Verbs

Other instances, people may want to give you specific directions. Therefore, they will tell you to turn left, walk one block, or keep on walking for half a mile.

Therefore, ensure you brush up on a number of these directional verbs you may hear.

Always remember that in the Spanish language, we have informal and formal ways of utilizing these directional verbs. Check out some of these examples:

Vos or tu- informal forms of you

Usted- formal

Let us discuss the tu that is the most form of the verb a lot of people utilize when providing direction on the road or street. You may hear them using these directional verbs such as this:

- *Gira a la izqueirda- turn left*
- *Gira a la derecha- turn right*
- *Ve por- walk or take long*
- *Cruza- cross*
- *Sigue- continue*
- *Sigue derecho- Go straight ahead*

There is a public transport

When you ask is it far or "**¿Está lejos?**" and the reply is Si, you may have to take public transport. Someone may say to you:

- Toma- take
- El autobus- the buss

- El metro- subway
- El train- the train
- Un taxi – a taxi

Adverbs of Place and Location

In Spanish, adverbs are invariable, which is, they don't show gender or number. The role is to alter the meaning of adjectives and verbs and the adverbs as well. Adverbs can be classified in many categories like time, manner, doubt, quantity, place, etc.

Adverbs of place are utilized to discuss the place of a thing or an action. They are specifically valuable for giving directions or expressing where people or items can be located.

Let's see some examples of adverbs of place:

- Abajo- downstairs, below
- Arriba- overhead, upstairs, above
- aquí, acá -here, over here
- ahí, allá- over there,there
- adentro- inside
- afuera- outside
- detras- after, behind
- ante- before
- lejos- far away
- cerca- near, close, nearby
- delante- ahead of
- enfrente- in front of
- fuera- outside
- dentro- inside

Adverbial of Locations

Here are some examples of adverbs of locations:

- En casa- at home
- A casa- to home
- A la derecha- to the right
- A la izquierda- to the left
- de arriba hacia abajo- downward
- de abajo hacia arriba- upward
- dentro de- inside, within
- fuera de- outside, without

- en alguna parte- somewhere
- en cualquier parte- anywhere
- en el extranjero- abroad
- en cualquier momento- whenever, at any time
- en ninguna parte- nowhere
- al revés-backwards
- en todas parter- everywhere
- en otra parte- elsewhere
- por ahí- over there, that way
- por aquí- over here, this way

Sample Exercises

The bank is behind that building- Detrás de ese edificio está el banco.

People like to eat well everywhere in the world- En todas partes del mundo, a la gente le gusta comer bien

Additional Notes

In Spanish, adverbial locations are specific phrasal expressions which make use of adverbs. The lists of adverbs of place above aren't comprehensive. On the other hand, they must give a good idea of the whole formation and use. Adverbs of place find the action of the verb associated with the space that it happens. Think about the phrase caminamor, or we walk. What many people know from this is the action, the actor and the time when it happens, when you don't know where it happens. The adverb of place describes this place to make the action of verbs descriptive as well as more precise. As a result, you can say we walk behind the guide or caminamos detras de la quia that provides verbal act a sense of spatiality.

TIP: *Usually, if you ask for a direction, you will not totally comprehend the answer, just keep in mind the first two or three things people say.*

Using Command Form to Give Directions

When giving directions in Spanish, most likely you will be utilizing the mandato or command. If you are not totally familiar with Spanish commands, you don't have to worry. These commands are easy to conjugate and have few irregularities.

Check this quick refresher regarding Spanish commands:

In Spanish languages, there are four basic forms of the command, such as:

- Tu form- informal singular
- Usted form- formal singular
- Vosotros form- informal plural
- Ustedes form- formal form

Keep in mind that vosotros is just utilized in Spain, in countries in Latin America, they use ustedes to talk to a group of people, in spite of the formality of the situation. When providing directions, perhaps you will just give affirmative commands like telling them what to do.

Commands in the form of tu are similar to the ella, el, usted form of the present simple.

come

Come! (Eat!)- comer (to eat)

¡Camina! (Walk!)- Caminar (to walk)

¡Abre! (Open!)- abrir (to open)

To form commands in the form of vosotros, just eliminate the r at the last part of the infinitive and put in a d:

Take a look at the examples below:

¡Comed! (Eat!) – come (to eat)

¡Caminad! (Walk!)-*Caminar* (to walk)

¡Abrid! (Open!)-*Abrir* (to open)

Commands in the form of usted are similar to the el, ella, usted form of the present subjunctive. Take a look at the examples below:

¡Coma! (Eat!)-*Comer* (to eat)

¡Camine! (Walk!)-*Caminar* (to walk)

¡Abra! (Open!)- *Abrir* (to open)

To forms command in the form of ustedes, make use of the ellos, ellas as well as usteded from of the present subjective. Here are some examples:

¡Coman! (Eat!)-*Comer* (to eat)

¡Caminen! (Walk!)- *Caminar* (to walk)

¡Abran! (Open!)-*Abrir* (to open)

Important Tip: *The verbs mentioned are regular in the command form, except for Ir. The tu form of ir is ve, while vaya in usted form, id in vosotros form as well as vayan in ustedes form.*

14 Key Phrases for Receiving and Giving Directions in the Spanish Language

Now that we have gone over important words and assessed verb conjugations, let us practice placing it all to make some key phrases related to direction.

Here are some of the best examples:

I'm lost- Estoy perdido/a.

- Excuse me, I'm lost. Can you help me?- Disculpe, estoy perdida. ¿Me puedes ayudar?
- Where is...- Dónde está...
- Where is Retiro Park?- ¿Dónde está el parque de Retiro?
- I'm looking for...- **Estoy buscando...**
- I'm looking for Flower Street- *Estoy buscando la calle Flores.*
- Is there a good restaurant around here?- *Hay un buen restaurante por aquí?*
- Is it close/far away?- *¿Está cerca/lejos?*
- Is July 9th Avenue far away?- *¿Está lejos la avenida 9 de Julio?*

Providing Directions

- Continue straight - **Sigue recto**
- Continue straight until the stoplight- *Sigue recto hasta el semáforo.*
- Follow _____ Avenue - **Sigue la avenida _____.**

Of course, you can replace avenida for other the same words such as calle, or street, callejon or alleyway, carretera or highway, Puente or bridge. Always keep in mind that in Spanish, not like in English, phrases like these, in general, come before the street of the name, rather than after.

Like for instance, when a street was named Teresa Street in English, in Spanish, it will be called calle Teresa.

More examples:

- *Follow Chile Avenue- Sigue la avenida de Chile*
- *Turn left or right- Gira/**dobla a la derecha/izquierda***
- ***When you arrive at the peak, turn right-*** *Cuando llegues al parque, gira a la derecha.*
- Go/walk/drive until the _____. - ***Ve/camina/conduce hasta*** _____.
- Walk until the gym and turn left- *Camina hasta el gimnasio y gira a la izquierda.*
- Take the first right/left. - ***Toma la primera derecha/izquierda.***

Surely, you can also replace primera or first for segunda or second or tercera or third according to your needs.

Check out the examples below:

- Continue straight, and take the second left- *Sigue recto, y toma la segunda izquierda.*
- It's on the right/left. - ***Está a la derecha/izquierda.***
- The bank is on Main Street. It's on the right- *El banco está en la calle principal. Está a la derecha.*
- It's next to _____. - ***Está al lado de*** _____.

Esta plus a preposition plus a place is a formula which you can utilize to describe the place of something which is relative to other locations. Take a look at these example phrases:

- My house is across from the school - *Mi casa está en frente de la escuela.*
- It's _____ minutes away- ***Está a*** _____ ***minutos.***
- It's not far. It's ten minutes away on foot. - *No está lejos. Está a diez minutos caminando.*
- It's _____ blocks/miles/kilometers away. - ***Está a*** _____ ***cuadras/manzanas/millas/kilómetros***

Practice Recommendation for Learning Your Spanish Directions

Here are easy, DIY exercises to learn directions in Spanish or just to restore your memory.

Writing Practice- This can help you concentrate on learning as well as memorizing the vocabulary words that are associated with directions in Spanish. It is very easy and straightforward- pick two locations in your city or vicinity, and write how to get from one to the other.

Listening and Speaking Practice: Choose to practice Spanish directions with your friends or loved ones? This is Spanish vocabulary exercise is ideal for you.

Look for a map and a friend. Pick a starting point on the map and then mark it. Then, without telling your buddy what it is, pick an endpoint. Explain to your friend or buddy, in as many details as possible on how from the very beginning till end. Switch off to practice listening and speaking.

Comprehension practice: Today, people are becoming reliant on phones and devices to get them from one point to another. Feeling sure and positive in your abilities in the Spanish language? Switch your device into Spanish when utilizing the maps application. You are able to practice your reading comprehension with a walking direction and switch on the navigation to perform comprehension during trips.

Knowing how to receive and give Spanish directions is perhaps a valuable thing you are able to have when you are travelling. Imagine getting confused in an odd place and don't the way to your hotel. This is an overwhelming scenario. However, if you are able to speak basic Spanish directions, then there is no need for you to worry about. The most excellent way to become proficient in Spanish directions is to practice a lot.

Animals (Farm, Forest & Sea)

Everyone loves animals. It serves as our stress reliever. Even when you have never had a pet before, perhaps you have watched the strange documentary on your favorite animal show. Animals when t comes to the conversation a universal topic. The list below must prepare you for a conversation with virtually any animal or pet lover.

Is it a Girl or a Boy? Animal and Gender in the Spanish Language

Prior to knowing animal's vocabulary in Spanish, there is a grammar point one must be wary of. In Spanish, nouns can be masculine or feminine. This disparity can frequently seem irrational and unsound to those who can't speak Spanish. Like for example, La Mesa or a table is feminine, while el escritorio or a desk is masculine.

Therefore, what occurs with animals? Most names of animal have a male and female form, however not all. Like for example, a cat can be a la gata which is in feminine form or el gato in a masculine form. On the other hand, a hamster will always be in a masculine form (el hamster).

It is very vital for you to know that biological gender and grammatical gender are not always alike or the same.

In Spanish, masculine is normally the default gender. Like for instance, if referring to many dogs, a Spanish people will say los perro (masculine form), in spite of whether a lot of dogs in that group are females or female.

Having said that, sometimes feminine can be utilized as a generic gender. If portraying a group of turtles, a Spanish person prefers to say in a feminine form which is las Tortugas before in the masculine form which is los tortugos. You can just utilize the second one when you are certain that in that group of turtles, most are males.

The list of animals below takes account of the generic form, which is to say, one you will make use of if you are not sure if the gender is male or female. So, let check this out!

LAS MASCOTAS (PETS)

Do you love dog, cat, rabbit or any types of animals? In spite of what kind of animals you prefer, pets are frequently the best place to begin a conversation concerning animals. Know the name of your pets in Spanish by checking this list:

- Dog- el perro
- Puppy- el cachorro
- Cat- el gato
- Hamster- el hamster
- Guinea Pig- La cobaya
- Fish- el pez
- Bird- el pajaro
- Turtle- la Tortuga
- Parakeet- el perico
- Snake- la serpiente

Let us check these popular phrases:

- I am going to walk the dog- *Voy a pasear el perro*
- My cat is white- Mi *gato es blanco.*
- That turtle doesn't eat lettuce- *Esa tortuga no come lechuga.*

LA GRANJA (THE FARM)

Do you love spending your extra time in the countryside? The names of animals listed below may come in handy:

- Rabbit- el conejo
- Chick/ chicken- el pollito/ el pollo
- Hen- la gallina
- Rooster- El gallo
- Cow- La vaca
- Bull- el toro
- Sheep- la oveja
- Horse- el caballo
- El Puerco/ el cerdo- pig
- Goat- la cabra
- Donkey- el burro
- Mouse- el raton

You may use these names of animals in the following sentences:

- Let's go milk the cows- *Vamos a ordeñar las vacas*
- I like to ride a horse- *Me gusta montar a caballo.*
- The sheep eat grass- *Las ovejas comen pasto.*
-

EL BOSQUE (THE FOREST)

There are lots of animals in the forest. Let's take a look at some of the common animals found in the forest and their names in Spanish.

- Deer- el ciervo
- Raccoon- el mapache
- Squirrel- la ardilla
- Owl- el buho
- Fox- El zorro
- Wolf- el lobo
- Bear- el oso
- El oso – Bear

You can mention them in sentences like these:

- The owl is in the tree- *El búho está en el árbol.*
- The squirrel eats nuts- *La ardilla come nueces.* -
- The bear sleeps- *El oso duerme*
- The owl is flying- el búho está volando
- The wolf is big- el lobo es grande

EL OCÉANO (THE OCEAN)

Love spending quality time in the sea? There may be instances that you may run into these sea animals:

- Crab- El cangrejo
- Jellyfish- La medusa/El aguaviva
- Dolphin- El delfín
- Whale- La ballena
- Shark- El tiburón
- Seal- La foca
- Sea lion- El lobo marino
- Walrus- La morsa
- Penguin- El pingüino

You can use these in the sentence like:

- There are lots of jellyfish- *Hay muchas medusas-*
- Look out, a shark! - *¡Cuidado, un tiburón!* -
- The sea lions eat fish- *Los lobos marinos comen pescado.*
- I want to see a sea lion in person- quiero ver un lobo marino en persona

EN EL ZOOLÓGICO (AT THE ZOO)

Want to see some exotic animals. Well, most of them can be found at the zoo. Below are some of the common names of exotic animals in Spanish.

- Elephant- El elefante
- Rhinoceros- El rinoceronte
- Hippopotamus- El hipopótamo
- Lion- El león
- Tiger- El tigre
- Giraffe- La jirafa
- Zebra- La cebra
- Monkey- El mono
- Kangaroo- El canguro
- Crocodile- El cocodrilo

Let' us check some of the phrases regarding exotic animals in Spanish.

- Elephants have a good memory- *Los elefantes tienen buena memoria.*
- Elephants are the biggest animals in the world- los elefantes son los animales más grandes del mundo
- Lions are the kings of the jungle- *El león es el rey de la selva.* -
- Kangaroos live in Australia- *Los canguros viven en Australia.*
- The monkey has a baby- el mono tiene un bebe

INSECTOS E BICHOS (INSECTS AND BUGS)

They may not be the first think that comes to your mind when you talk about animals. However, for some, they may not even something they like to think of at all. Insects and bugs are almost everywhere. Therefore, it is very vital to become aware of their terms in Spanish. Let's check this out!

- Caterpillar- La oruga
- Butterfly- La mariposa
- Moth- la polilla
- Fly- La mosca
- Spider- la arana
- Cockroach- la curacha
- Snail- El caracol
- Worm- El gusano

Let us use this in the sentence:

- Butterflies are colorful- *Las mariposas son coloridas.*
- Spiders scare me- *Las arañas me dan miedo.*
- There is a snail on the plant- *Hay un caracol en la planta.* -

Making Use of the Personal A with Animals

Even if the personal A is usually utilized with a human being, it can also be utilized with animals like pets which the Spanish speaker has a strong attachment to. Keep in mind the difference in the sentences given below:

I saw a dog with just one eye- Vi un perro con un solo ojo. Here the Spanish speaker is referring to an otherwise unidentified dog.

The veterinarian euthanized my 9-year-old dog- El veterinario sacrificó a mi perra de nueve años. Here, the Spanish refer to a pet which he believes thinks of as a personality.

The above list covers many grounds, on the other hand. Still, there is a big part of the animal kingdom left that you have to explore.

Learning Adjectives, Attributes & Clothing in Spanish

If you are going to choose, would you prefer watching a black and white show, or a high-quality standard, or a full-colored one?

I am sure that you are going to pick a full-colored movie since it is closer, more exciting, and more interesting in terms of a real-life situation.

If you are going to learn the Spanish language without the usage of an adjective, then you might consider it as you were watching a black and white movie version. Yes, we are all aware that you can get the idea of the movie even if it is on a black and white version, but we can't deny the fact that you can feel boringness.

During your childhood days, you are knowledgeable about telling your parents what you feel – either sad or happy or saying that someone is nice or a little bit mean. You usually see various things in black and white colors since you don't have the entire and colorful coloring materials.

The crayons in this article refer to the adjectives in Spanish. If you are knowledgeable about the basic Spanish terms, but you can't still describe a particular thing correctly, then you are at the right place. In this post, we will provide you with some of the adjectives in Spanish – that was translated into English, that you should know.

Noun-Adjective Agreements in Spanish

We are all aware in the saying that "in love, opposites attract." Well, in Spanish, it was different, since every word must agree with each other. There will be no mix-matched and fighting pairs. It only means that you are required to use nouns in Spanish that will agree with the adjectives that you will use. If you prefer a feminine noun, then you should look for an adjective that is feminine as well.

All the adjectives that have –o in the end usually have 4 different endings – ne for plural, singular, feminine, and masculine. Maintain the –o at the end of a masculine adjective, and switch it into the letter –a when used with feminine adjectives. If you want to make an adjective plural, add letter –s at every end of letters –a and –o.

Examples

> The tall girl – "*La chica alta.*"

"Girl" is a feminine noun. Thus the adjective "tall" must be in the feminine form.

The red car – "*El coche rojo.*"

The noun "car" is considered masculine; thus, the adjective "red" must be in the masculine form.

This is also similar to plural adjectives and plural nouns. If you use a plural noun, then you are also required to change the used adjective into its plural form.

Examples

The red cars – "*Los coches rojos*"

The tall girls – "*Las chicas altas*"

This can also be used if your preferred adjective does not come up after the usage of the noun in the sentence.

Example

The man is tall – "*El hombre es alto.*"

Even though the placement of es – as a verb is in the middle of two, the alto – as an adjective is still being used to refer the hombre – as a noun, thus the noun and the adjective must agree with each other.

For your information, some of the adjectives are not in the masculine and feminine form. Some of these maintain their spellings and usage.

All the adjectives that have the ending of –ista or –e do not switch their versions into either feminine or masculine. If you are going to use this kind of Spanish adjective, then you are required not to change it.

Examples

My grandpa is idealistic – "*Mi abuelo es idealista.*"

My grandma is idealistic – "*Mi abuela es idealista.*"

The sad girl – "*La chica triste.*"

The sad day – "*El día triste.*"

Notice that all of the used adjectives above did not alter the spelling of its ending. On the other hand, you are still required to put letter –s at the end of the adjectives to turn it into its plural form.

Examples

>   The girls are sad – *"Las chicas están tristes."*

>   My grandparents are idealistic – *"Mis abuelos son idealistas."*

The similar rule is also being used in some adjectives that usually end with the consonant letters, but, with some exclusions.

Examples

>   The blue shirt – *"La camiseta azul."*

>   The blue car – *"El coche azul."*

If you prefer using the adjective on its plural form, then you are required to add –es on its end.

Example

>   The blue shirts – *"Las camisetas azules."*

On the other hand, if the consonant –z is at the end of an adjective, then you are required to turn it into the letter –c before changing it into its plural form.

Examples

>   The girls are happy – *"Las chicas son felices."*

>   The girl is happy – *"La chica es feliz."*

Where is the Proper Placement of an Adjective in a Spanish Sentence?

This time that you are aware of making your basic adjective into a colorful one, the next thing that you should know is where to put them properly?

The only answer is very easy to follow – place your preferred adjective right after the position of your used noun. But in real-life, the placement is much more complicated.

Qualifying adjectives typically follow after the used noun.

These are the adjectives that are being used in describing the nationalities or even the physical characteristics of a person. These usually come from various verbs.

Examples

A black table – *"Una mesa negra."*

An English man – *"Un hombre inglés."*

Adjectives in Spanish that are Considered Identifiers are being placed before the Position of Noun

All the identifying Spanish adjectives include the so-called demonstrative adjectives, including that (*aquel*) and this *(este.)* The demonstrative adjectives are usually placed go before the Spanish noun. This rule is alsotrue in terms of possessive adjectives, which is usually used to refer someone who owns a particular thing, such as our or nuestro and my or mi in Spanish.

If you are going to use a limiting adjective, then you should also place it prior to the position of a noun. This kind of adjective is one of the adjectives that will limit the quantity of a noun.

Examples;

I have enough time – *"Tengo suficiente tiempo."*

In this example, the adjective used was enough or suficiente in Spanish. Since it will limit the time or tiempo in Spanish, it is a must for you to place it before a noun. This rule is also used in terms of using numbers.

Spanish adjectives that will give you emotional impacts, or will release essential qualities must be written preceding the noun inside a sentence.

Examples;

The brave general – *"El valiente general."*

In this example, placing the Spanish word valiente first emphasize the term brave and is usually defines as the emotional characteristic.

He or she is a good friend – *"Es un buen amigo."*

In this example, a friend is good, which means he or she does good things to you and vice versa, instead of putting a "good" individual.

Spanish Adjectives That Alter the Meaning of a Sentence Based on its Placement

Yes, what you read is right. Some of the Spanish adjectives that you will encounter may change the meaning of your sentence because of its placement – whether you placed it after or before the placement of a noun.

Placing the Spanish adjective prior to the noun is usually completed for the addition of subjective feelings or emotional resonance, instead of using an objective fact.

Example;

> The poor woman – *"La pobre mujer."*

In this example, the speaker was touched because of the situation of the woman; it is considered as more than just a state of a human being compared to the financial fact.

The woman has little money – *"La mujer pobre."*

On the other hand, this example is considered as an objective fact in a sentence.

I have a longtime friend – *"Tengo un viejo amigo."*

I have an old friend – *"Tengo un amigo Viejo"* – the friend who was being pointed in this sentence has an old age.

Placing the Spanish term "Viejo" or old in English after the term amigo or friend shows that he has a longtime or old friend. Om the other hand, putting it before the term amigo shows that the age of his friend was old.

The following are some of the Spanish adjectives that will change the meaning of a sentence varying upon their placement.

- Grande or gran – putting the Spanish adjective gran or grande after the noun means "big or large." But, putting it before the noun means "excellent or great."
- Nuevo – putting the Spanish adjective "Nuevo" after the noun means "new." On the other hand, putting it prior to the placement of a noun means "different."
- Varios – putting the Spanish term "varios" in front of a noun means "varied." But, placing it before the placement of a Spanish noun means "several."

- Único – placing the Spanish term "único" after the Spanish noun means "varied." However, if you will place it before the placement of a Spanish noun, it will mean "only."
- Cierto – If you will place the Spanish word "cierto" after a Spanish noun, it means "correct or right." But, if you are going to place it before the usage of a Spanish noun, it will mean as "certain."
- Alto – if you will put the Spanish word "alto" after the placement of a Spanish noun, it means "tall." On the other hand, if you will place it before using a noun in a sentence, it means "top quality."

We recommend you to use these Spanish adjectives in a sentence and determine what your sentence means when you place these after and before the usage of a Spanish noun.

How to Learn Spanish Attributes

Some of you see the world as a black and white movie. Well, we can't blame you with that. But, let us tell you something, our world is much more colorful and vibrant compared to what you think.

Even though malo and Bueno are considered as enough adjective-wise that can fix a sentence, separating our entire earth into bad and good would not only give boringness to those who are listening to you but, it will also limit your words.

But, if you are a type of person who gets worried about knowing and understanding the Spanish adjectives and attributes as a strain on your brain and very time-consuming, well we recommend you to throw away those thoughts from your mind.

For your information, some of the ordinary Spanish adjectives are closely similar to their counterparts in the English language. Because of that, it is not only the reason for learning with the common adjectives in Spanish and determining their meanings in the English language.

What is the Importance of Learning the Various Adjectives in Spanish?

Learning various languages is all about showing things on yourself, and it is similar in explaining your feelings and thoughts on some kinds of cases, people, places, films, and objects with the huge loads of languages. This is the real reason for you to at least understand and learn some of the Spanish adjectives that will define your physical attributes.

Adjectives – whether Spanish or English also add variety, interest, and color to our world, which helps you to express yourself and feel even better.

Where Should You Place a Spanish Adjective in a Sentence?

The proper order of the usage of Spanish adjectives is the number one problem of those who are just starting to learn Spanish adjectives and attributes. If you are one of them, keep in mind that dissimilar in the English language, the adjectives in Spanish are usually being placed after the usage of a noun. So, rather than saying "she possesses the beautiful pair of blue eyes," why not say the equivalent sentence, which is "she possess the pair of eyes blue beautiful" or *tiene unos ojos azules preciosos* in Spanish.

You might say that it has a weird sound, but, when you already get the thought of the sentence, placing a noun right before the usage of an adjective will flow on you naturally.

On the other hand, do not forget that some of the Spanish adjectives can e either pliral and singular or feminine and masculine. So, the Spanish term "lindo" can be written as lindas for feminine plural, lindos for masculine plural, linda for feminine singular, and lindo for masculine singular. But, keep in mind that a Spanish adjective that you are going to use must agree with the noun that it modifies.

It only means that if you will be talking with a person using a feminine, plural noun, such as words or palabras, you had to need to feminine and plural adjective.

For instance, "what a beautiful words!" in Spanish, *"¡Qué lindas palabras!"*

Common Adjectives in Spanish that will help you to Describe Things Around You

- Pretty – *Lindo*

Can you still recall those blue pair of beautiful eyes that she possesses? They are so pretty or *¡Qué lindos que son* in Spanish.

- Ugly – *Feo*

There is no doubt that there is no one in this world that will talk about the ugly pair of eyes, but we can't deny the fact that there is a lot of things in this world that are considered as *feo*. These feo things might include the performance, behavior, or appearance of something or someone.

- Happy – *Feliz*

Similar to the Pharrell Williams, can you recall the alteration between the usage of the Spanish term "Soy feliz " or "I am a happy person" and "estoy feliz" or "I am temporarily happy? Pharrell will always be present.

- Sad – *Triste*

There is no individual in this world that feels happy on his or her entire life. We all experience sadness, and that is part of our lives.

"We all feel sad when Pharrell's song is over" or *"Todos nos sentimos tristes cuando termina la canción de Pharrell"* in English.

- Tall – *Alto*

At this part, we are going to tackle some of the Spanish adjectives that you can use to describe a physical attribute of a person.

For instance, "some girls are tall, and some are not" or *"Algunas chicas son altas y otras no"* in Spanish. In this example, we had used the Spanish plural feminine adjective, which is "altas."

- Short – *Bajo*

Everybody differs from each other. Thus, it is a must for you to understand and learn how to describe a wide array of various traits.

For example, "" people who have short height are cute" or *"las personas que tienen estatura baja son lindas"* in Spanish.

- Big – *Grande*

Similar to the smile of Pharrell, it is big or grande. Keep in mind that adjectives that are usually ending with the letter "e" will always be the same for both feminine and masculine nouns.

For instance, "he has a very big tummy, and I think that is cute" or *"él tiene una grande barriga y creo que es lindo"* in Spanish.

- Small – *Pequeño*

For example, "there is also a small area in his house" or *"también hay una pequeña área en su casa"* in Spanish.

- Simple – *Simple*

This is the Spanish adjective that is very simple to read and pronounce. It is just that you need to take a look at your proper pronunciation to this adjective. Dissimilar to the English language, the Spanish terms, nouns, and adjectives, have their stresses at every start of the term. On the other hand, in English, you will pronounce this adjective as "sim-PLE or SimPULL," while in Spanish, you will pronounce it as SIM-ple or Seem-pley, wherein the stress is at the beginning of the first syllable.

The Spanish adjective "simple" also connotes the term "lacking" or "bland" in something, most notably when you will describe a food.

- Complicated – *Complicado*

Generally, it is not complicado for you to absorb and use these Spanish adjectives in a sentence.

- Fun – *Divertido*

For instance, "Learning Spanish language will give you so much fun" or *"aprender español te dará mucha divertido"* in the Spanish language.

Similar to other English terms, including "happy," whether you will use Spanish terms, like estar or ser prior to the usage of this adjective, the placement of the adjective can impact the meaning of your composed sentence.

Juan is fun or *Juan es divertido* in Spanish.

The example mentioned above only means that the person, who is Juan, was described as a fun individual. Keep in mind that ser is being used in talking about the general cases, things, or properties that are considered as true.

On the other hand, the phrase "Juan esta divertido hoy" or *Juan is fun today* in English proposes that he is not fun every time except *today.* The usage of the Spanish term *estar* in this example emphasizes the impermanent nature of aa person, who is Juan, for being a fun individual to be with.

- Boring – *Aburrido*

If you are a type of person who is thinking that learning Spanish adjectives is boring, then let me tell you that you are wrong.

For instance, "there is no boring item in this world" or *no hay artículo aburrido en este mundo* in Spanish.

Take note that the usage of estar and ser is being used in modifying the meanings of an adjective, but it can also give you various meanings: someone or something that can be bored or *está aburrido* or can be boring or *es aburrido.*

- Rich – *Rico*

This Spanish term is generally being used when you are talking with wealthy families or individuals.

For instance, "her family is rich" or *su familia es rica.*"

The Spanish term *rico* can also be used if you will describe a food. For example, "the food he served to us was delicious" or *la comida que nos sirvió estaba rico.*"

Take note that various usage of estar and ser can give you different meanings varying upon their placement. You have got the first example emphasizing the wealth of a family, and the second one is the temporary savor that was being perceived at a period.

- Poor – *Pobre*

Similar in the English language, you can also tackle about a person that is poor, which means he or she does not have any penny on his or her pocket.

For example, "the boy is very poor" or *la chica es muy pobre.* You can also use this Spanish adjective in an expression of sympathy or exclamation for a particular individual.

For instance, "poor boy!" or *pobre chico.*

In this example, it suggests that he won't have a good time anymore, even though he is considered as rica in terms of richness.

- Delicious – *delicioso*

Aside from using the Spanish adjective *rico,* you can also use *delicioso* as your adjective when describing the taste of a food or dish.

- Disgusting – *Repugnante*

The Spanish adjective *repugnante* is considered as a strong term that you can use in a sentence. Yofor additional effect, you can also use yur disgusted face when saying this term.

For example, "you have a disgusting scent" or *tienes un olor repugnante* in Spanish.

- Intelligent – *Inteligente*

You are not required to be an *inteligente* person to understand the basic Spanish terms and adjectives.

- Stupid – *Tonto*

Aside from the Spanish adjective *tonto,* you can also use the term *estúpido* in a sentence. But the latter is not usually being used in a sentence.

- New – *Nuevo*

This Spanish adjective is very self-explanatory.

- Old – *Viejo*

It is also common to use *los viejos* in referring your old parents, but we know that they might not love hearing that.

This Spanish adjective is not considered as being rude or offensive term, but, it will always vary upon the one who you are describing at.

- Open – *Abierto*

Similar to its English counterpart, open, you can use abierto in describing an individual. For example, "he or she is a very open person" or *Es una persona muy abierta* in Spanish.

You can also use it if you are going to describe an establishment or a shop. For example, "the company where I work was open for 12 hours" or *la empresa donde trabajo estuvo abieta durante 12 horas.*

Again, keep in mind the alteration of the usage of the verbs estar and ser.

- Closed – *Cerrado*

You can also take an establishment or a company as an example in this Spanish adjective. An establishment can close late depending on the area where it was located.

For example, "the company where I work was closed during 1 in the afternoon and opened at 8 in the morning" or *"La empresa donde trabajo estaba cerrada durante la 1 de la tarde y abre a las 8 de la mañana."*

- Tired – *Cansado*

Some people are being confused between the word casado and cansado, wherein casado means married, and cansado means tired. For example, "she feels tired in theor relationship, so she broke up with him" or *ella se siente cansada en su relación, así que rompió con él* in Spanish.

- Awake – *Despierto*

For example, "her baby was awake, thus she needs to give him some milk" or *su bebé estaba despierto, por lo que necesita darle un poco de leche* in Spanish.

- Hot – *Caluroso*

For example, "one of the reasons why babies are wake during nighttime because it was too hot" or *Una de las razones por las cuales los bebés están despiertos durante la noche porque hacía demasiado caluroso* in Spanish.

- Cold – *Frio*

You can use this Spanish adjective when you are referring to the lower temperatures that you see on a thermometer. For example, "Some people prefer cold weather, that is why they go to cold countries such as Antarctica" or *algunas personas prefieren el clima frío, por eso van a países fríos como la Antártida* in Spanish.

- Expensive – *Caro*

For example, do rich countries also manufacture and supply *caro* gadgets and other items?

- Barato – *Cheap*

For example, "one of the reasons behind the popularity of candies is that these are so *barato*

- Fast – *Rápido*

For instance, you will be able to learn the Spanish language rápido if you have a knowledgeable and effective mentor

- Slow – *Lento*

For instance, some people prefer riding in a *lento* vehicle for them to enjoy the beauty of the country they visited

- Crazy – *Loco*

For example, in these days, ladies fell in love with those men who have *loco* personality compared to those good-looking ones.

- Tranquil – *Tranquilo*

The Spanish adjective *tanquilo* can also be used as an order or suggestion, furthermore to its meaning as "tranquil" or "calm."

For example, if you are going to tell someone who is working up with a sentence with the use of the Spanish adjective *tranquilo,* it only means that you are saying that they need to be relaxed. It is also a good way for you to tell this with a reassuring and calming voice.

- Strong – *Fuerte*

For instance, a man who usually goes to their gym area gets fuerte body and larger muscles compared to those who didn't.

- Weak – Débil

For example, she feels so débil when she sees a snake and a frog.

- Sick – *Enfermo*

There are times that you will feel a little *enfermo* when you try to push yourself performing heavy exercises. Thus, you need to take some rest.

- Healthy – *Sano*

I know that you are aware that the Spanish adjective "sano" can also be linked to the term "sane" in terms of emotional and mental health of a person. In some ways, this is considered as a positive or a compliment to a person.

- Sweet – *Dulce*

The Spanish adjective "dulce" is not all about savor, and it can also be used by some people in giving his or her compliment to a thing or a person.

For instance, you have a very sweet personality, and I think I like it or *Tienes una personalidad muy dulce y creo que me gusta* in Spanish.

If you are talking about the sticky and sweet bun beside the person you are communicating with, you can say "está dulce," which is being used in describing the taste of the bun. Again, take note of the proper usage of *estar and ser* since its placement can change the meaning of your used adjective. It can turn to temporary savor of a meal from the permanent characteristic of a person.

- Savory – *Salado*

The Spanish adjective *salado* usually means "salty." But, it is generaly used in describing the taste of a dish. It is also being utilized in some colloquialisms in some parts of Latin America.

- Dirty – *Sucio*

For example, you are so dirty, get upstairs and clean yourself or *estás tan sucio, sube las escaleras y límpiate* in Spanish.

- Dry – *Seco*

For instance, I wish that tomorrow will be a dry day since my friends, and I have our seminars.

- Wet – *Mojado*

Mojado is the counterpart of Seco. It would be very helpful for you if you think that it will start to rain.

- Unfair – *Injusto*

Did your mother start ignoring you since your younger sibling was born? I know that its *injusto* but, take note that she still loves you.

- Fair - *Justo*

That feeling is not *justo* for you. You also need love and care from both of your parents.

- Empty – *Vasio*

That feeling of being *vasio* for your entire classes cause you didn't take your breakfast?

- Full – *Lleno*

When you write the things that you have been learned in your class, your notes will be lleno, and that will help you during your examinations.

- Thin – *Delgado*

People who have *Delgado* body are considered as slim, but some of those have baby fats which they cover with larger clothes.

- Good – *Bueno*

It would be *Bueno* for you if you will keep on reading this post until you memorized all the Spanish adjectives and attributes that you can use when talking in Spanish.

- Bad – *Malo*

Taking too many drugs and drinking a high amount of alcohol will give your body *malo* effects, most notably in your liver and kidneys.

CONCLUSION

(CONCLUSIÓN)

Learning a second language is not that easy but you have to admit that it is challenging. Aside from your native language, it is quite challenging to learn about a very unfamiliar language like the Spanish Language. *(Aprender un segundo idioma no es tan fácil, pero debes admitir que es un desafío. Además de su idioma nativo, es bastante difícil aprender sobre un idioma muy desconocido como el español.)*

Here, you have learned the correct pronunciation of some Spanish words, the proper gestures that must accompany the statement that you are making, and also the use of verbs, pronouns, nouns, adjectives, adverbs, prepositions and the like. Through this tool, you have learned all grammatical factors without enrolling in a formal class-type review of Spanish Language. *(Aquí, ha aprendido la pronunciación correcta de algunas palabras en español, los gestos adecuados que deben acompañar a la declaración que está haciendo, y también el uso de verbos, pronombres, sustantivos, adjetivos, adverbios, preposiciones y similares. A través de esta herramienta, ha aprendido todos los factores gramaticales sin inscribirse en una revisión formal de clase de español.)*

Furthermore, there are also short stories which make the learning even more exciting. Through some tips in reading, you will surely find Spanish Language reading and learning enjoyable instead of considering it as a burden. (Además, también hay historias cortas que hacen que el aprendizaje sea aún más emocionante. A través de algunos consejos en lectura, seguramente encontrará agradable la lectura y el aprendizaje del idioma español en lugar de considerarlo como una carga.)

The use of short stories may be considered as designed for kids or children who are learning through baby steps, but the truth is that a learner of second language is considered as baby steps too. There is no harm in considering it as a kid-like way of learning. That is again a form of humility. Remember that humility is the start of learning. *(El uso de cuentos cortos puede considerarse diseñado para niños o niños que están aprendiendo a través de pequeños pasos, pero la verdad es que un aprendiz de segundo idioma también se considera como pequeños pasos. No hay daño en considerarlo como una forma de aprendizaje infantil. Esa es nuevamente una forma de humildad. Recuerda que la humildad es el comienzo del aprendizaje.)*

As parting words, you should always carve in your mind that learning is one way of showing humility because you are admitting into yourself that you still have a lot to learn and that will make you even more fit to perfect your goal – in this instance, the Spanish Language and Grammar. *(Como palabras de despedida, siempre debes recordar que aprender es una forma de mostrar humildad porque admites en ti mismo que todavía tienes mucho que aprender y que te hará aún más apto para perfeccionar tu objetivo; en este caso, Lengua y gramática española.)*

CPSIA information can be obtained
at www.ICGtesting.com
Printed in the USA
BVHW090529110521
606944BV00004B/664